M000094719

THE OFFICE
GARDENER

OTHER BOOKS BY JACQUELINE HÉRITEAU

The How to Grow and Cook It Book
of Vegetables, Herbs, Fruits, and Nuts

Oriental Cooking
the Fast Wok Way

Take-It-Along Cookbook

The How to Grow and Can It Book
of Vegetables, Fruits, and Herbs

The Color Handbook of Houseplants
(*editor, with Elvin McDonald and Francesca Morris*)

The Good Housekeeping Illustrated
Encyclopedia of Gardening—16 volumes
(*editor, with Elvin McDonald*)

THE OFFICE GARDENER

by Jacqueline Hériteau

illustrated by Howard Berelson

HAWTHORN BOOKS, INC.
Publishers / NEW YORK

THE OFFICE GARDENER

Copyright © 1977 by Jacqueline Hériteau. Copyright under International and Pan-American Copyright Conventions. All rights reserved, including the right to reproduce this book or portions thereof in any form, except for the inclusion of brief quotations in a review. All inquiries should be addressed to Hawthorn Books, Inc., 260 Madison Avenue, New York, New York 10016. This book was manufactured in the United States of America and published simultaneously in Canada by Prentice-Hall of Canada, Limited, 1870 Birchmount Road, Scarborough, Ontario.

Library of Congress Catalog Card Number: 76–15765

ISBN: hardcover, 0–8015–5481–0; softcover, 0–8015–5482–9

1 2 3 4 5 6 7 8 9 10

To Richard Strain,
who helps people to grow and bloom

Contents

APPENDIXES   215

Foreword

Early in 1971 it became my awesome assignment to produce the sixteen-volume *Good Housekeeping Illustrated Encyclopedia of Gardening*. I was given eighteen months in which to assemble more than two million words and several thousand photographs and line drawings.

The first thing I did was to have lunch with Jacqueline Hériteau, mostly, I thought, to talk out my anxieties about the project. She reacted so positively that despite some misgivings about hiring such a close friend, I invited her to act as my general editor.

That very afternoon we went to look at the offices that awaited us and our staff. To put it politely, the furnishings were minimal. In fact, I thought the place was depressing, but Jacqui's opening remark was, "Look at all these windows—we can fill the place with plants!"

From that instant I felt a new confidence about my choice of general editor. Long ago I discovered that the individuals who grow plants in their work surroundings tend to be happier, more efficient, and easier to deal with than those who do not. Obviously, this is a grand generality, but in fact, plants are tremendously therapeutic. My own office is literally a breeding ground for tension. There are always more papers and pictures than I can stash neatly. And deadlines that usually seem impossible. But I've learned that a few minutes spent in caring for my office garden can be far more calming than smoking, having a drink, or popping a pill.

Our need for living plants in the rooms where we live has now been documented by such prestigious institutions as the Menninger Clinic in Topeka, Kansas, the Payne-Whitney Clinic in New York, and at the Institute of Rehabilitation Medicine at New York University Medical Center. If you have never thought consciously of your plants as being therapeutic, stop and spend some time with them the next time you feel work or personal stress, a period of the blues, or simply the need to get away from it all.

The 1970s have given us countless books about house plants. Now we have the first and much-needed guide to office plants. Whether you are the secretary responsible for the window box or the executive about to install an office jungle, you will find out everything you need to know in *The Office Gardener*.

Elvin McDonald

Acknowledgments

I am in debt to many friends and business associates for information pertaining to plants in office situations, particularly to associates who garden in climates warmer than those with which I am most familiar. My special thanks to Dagny Hansen of Plant Specialists, Inc., in New York City. Dagny started the company, one of the city's best indoor and outdoor landscapers. Dagny acted as consultant for this book, and many of the garden plans here are designs Dagny worked out for her clients. I also am most grateful to Norman Strain of Everett Conklin West, in East Irvine, California, a division of Everett Conklin, Inc., in New Jersey. Norman's firm designs and installs indoor gardens in malls and office buildings all over the country as well as in California, and he was most helpful in giving details of the plants that are both available and successful in his state and in the Southwest. I am also indebted to Elvin McDonald for information on flowering plants; to Kerry Fitzgerald, president of the City Gardener, New York landscapers; to Ruth Manning and Jerry Smith of Hunter Florists, Park Avenue, New York City; to Roger Caroll, consulting architect with the Port Authority of New York and New Jersey; and to industrial psychologist Lawrence Zeitlin of the City University of New York. And to Anne LeMoine for typing assistance.

I would like here to express my delight with Howard Berelson's handsome and accurate illustrations and to tell the world at large that the inspiration behind the book is Hawthorn editor Sandra Choron.

THE OFFICE
GARDENER

1
The Office Garden

Plants make you feel good. That's a fact. When there's new growth bursting out all over, everything fresh, green, and flourishing, the plants are little rockets of success going off every time you look at them. They make up for crowded elevators, crotchety bosses, grumpy partners, and mistakes somebody thinks you made. They even make up for mistakes you really did make. Flourishing plants are saying, "Here's something you did really right. You're terrific!" On the other hand, plants that do poorly have the reverse effect. Silly as it sounds, they really do add stress to your job.

There's no good reason for an office garden to be a flop. When I say "office garden," I don't mean the grounds of the Taj Mahal. An office garden can be anything from the geranium on your desk to a green corner in the reception area, to trees and shrubs an indoor landscaper installs in big work centers. The key to success in this—as in other challenges—is knowledge. So before you risk your pet pteris, enlarge the existing office plantings, or landscape with professional help, do your homework.

1 *Dieffenbachia 'Exotica'*; 2 *Ficus elastica decora;* 3 *Ficus lyrata;* 4 *Fatsia japonica*

Plants are like people: The ones you bring to work are looking for positions they can fill successfully. Conditions in most offices are significantly different from the conditions at home: Office environments are paradise to some, and to others, they're disaster.

For example, there are buildings whose lights burn day and night. This increases the footcandles of light delivered on a 24-hour basis, a benefit to plants such as the big fig trees, which may need more light than they normally get indoors in an 8-hour day. But night light is a bomb when Easter cactus is considered: Easter cactus can't bloom without a period of darkness. Other buildings cut off heat after five o'clock and during weekends. This is great for geraniums, which thrive on cool nights, but not so great for African violets, which flower best in even, warm temperatures.

So the first thing you need to consider when planning your office garden is whether the plants you have or want suit the situations you are offering; or, can the situations be altered to suit the plants?

Resumé: Plants at Work

The best plants for work areas are discussed in detail in chapters 2–6. These are the species and varieties professional interior landscapers recommend and use. They generally are tropicals, semitropicals, and desert plants—plants that grow well in the perpetual summer of the indoors. The plants listed here are easy to find and hard to kill. They present the lowest risk for the dollars invested and are among the most beautiful and useful of the plants that succeed indoors. You can add riskier and rarer plants to your work collection once your basic indoor garden is underway.

This hardy crew of working plants divides into five categories: small plants; shrubs; trees; vines and climbers; and flowering and fruiting plants. The first four categories deal with size. The last category contains plants of all sizes that add brilliant color and excitement to even the drabbest offices. But the most successful indoor plants are foliage plants. Indoor lighting isn't enough to keep most flowering and fruiting plants doing their thing.

When you are choosing plants for the office, you want to choose among plants that will do well there. But you also must choose plants that do their job—make the office beautiful. Not all plants are suited to all purposes. Plants, unlike Dresden china figures, are living, growing entities.

The small-plants category includes miniatures, dwarfs of larger species, low growers, young plants of fast-growing large species, and young plants of tall species that grow slowly. Young plants of fast-growing large species are apt to be among the least expensive plants at garden centers. That's nice if you are buying cheap to grow tall. However, fast-growing young plants aren't the best choice if you want a permanent plant for your desk, work tabletops, or washroom ledges. Miniatures, dwarfs, low growers, and slow growers are best in such places.

When considering smaller plants, you should know that several small plants are less effective in a large space than a few big plants and will probably take more time to care for on a weekly basis. Also, plants in small pots can become dangerously dry when the office closes for long weekends. You can offset this hazard by maneuvers such as tenting the plants during vacations, but maneuvering takes time. Have you got time?

Plants in the vining and climbing category come in various sizes, from babies with small leaves to the big-leafed philodendrons generally sold staked to bark-covered logs. Among vines and climbers are the good-looking basket plants. Vines and hanging baskets effectively soften barren corners, adorn dreary bookcases, and add charm to curtainless windows. The basket plants, however, are a nuisance to water unless you have a pulley installation, and even then they usually end up dripping water on the floor. Most vines and climbers must be pruned and pinched back to stay full. Realistically, the plants in this category are beautiful, but most take extra time in maintenance.

The most dramatic category of plants for work spaces— and the most expensive, too—are the large shrubs and trees. But match the cost of these against the cost of a lot of small plants and you get more garden for your money. Furthermore, maintenance is less time-consuming.

The most exciting plants of all are the flowering and fruiting plants, but darn it, the list is pretty small. As I said above, the lighting common to most work situations just isn't enough to keep flowers coming on most plants. Nevertheless, the present limited list will grow, because big business is beginning to move into the plant supply industry and money is being invested in developing more flowering and fruiting plants for indoors. You can bring color to the office in lots of ways if you want it badly enough, though. Seasonal flowers from the florist and wild bouquets from country weekends are one way to keep color around you. Yet another is to strategically spot bouquets of colorful dried flowers among the foliage plants.

Situations Wanted: The Office Climate

Will *your* office light support plants? The answer, particularly if it is in a modern building, is a wholehearted yes! If yours isn't a modern building, today there are ways to provide the kind of light plants need without too much trouble or cost.

Modern offices are looking more like gardens because light sources in these buildings make indoor gardens so successful. The cozy, dim interiors of Sherlock Holmes's day—a little fire whispering on the boss's hearth, gaslight, and the scratching of a quill pen—can't raise a decent mushroom, let alone support cascades of strawberry begonias. If you've been resenting the glass-sheathed monument to the future that shelters your labors and hating the glare of its fluorescent corridors, don't. Just think greenhouse. The charm of the past may be missing, but the lighting and temperatures that plants respond to are there—everywhere, not just on a few windowsills.

About 90 percent of the lighting in the new buildings is based on combinations of fluorescents, including one cool and one warm white light. This will support most everything you love, from a fan palm to a potful of variegated pothos.

They'll support it so well that in fact I know of one company moving from New York to the Midwest that almost succeeded in selling its magnificent office garden back to the landscaper who installed it. (The landscaper had to say no because the plants had become so monumental over the years that they were impractical to move.) I have also heard that some interior landscapers in the northern climates will rent plants for the winter to large civic centers for practically nothing because the offices make such good cold-weather storage places.

Even if fluorescents of this sort aren't available, you can grow plants at work. Windowsill gardens are usually successful in offices, and there are among the plants in this book a few that will grow joyfully in the dimmer light of interior corners. But more exciting is the appearance on the market of various styles of individual spotlights and grow lights that support plants so well. These can be placed anywhere and work very well in my experience.

There are experts who have had equal success with spotlights and floodlights containing ordinary incandescent bulbs! They say it is the quantity rather than the quality of light that counts.

As for problems particular to modern buildings, there are ways out. For instance, when dealing with lights that are cut off nights and weekends, choose plants suited to these conditions (see chapters 2 through 6). Other solutions to other problems and ways to capitalize on the light assets you have are discussed in Chapter 8.

Temperatures aren't a problem for plants in most offices. The plants we are accustomed to growing indoors are those that grow in the climate best suited for people—65 to 70 degrees. Since modern offices either heat or air-condition to offset any outdoor deviation from that comfortable zone, indoor temperatures are as ideal as a Caribbean island for plants.

Where you might have cause for concern about temperatures for your office plants is in buildings in which heat or air conditioning are turned off at five o'clock and on weekends, but the temperature drop would have to be extreme to matter—below 55 degrees and over 75 degrees for most of the plants in this book.

The adaptability of plants is your ally—it never fails to surprise me. Some years ago I arrived at work one Monday morning in late spring to find a window wide open and traces of snow from a freaky spring storm. There were my ferns and begonias and geraniums right near the window in a freezing-cold room. Yet of the lot, I lost only one.

Salary Requirements: Maintenance for Office Plants

Watering, feeding, grooming, occasional potting, pinching and pruning vining plants—these are the sum of the maintenance chores required to keep office plants looking beautiful. An infestation of pests or disease attack is something else again. Chapter 8 discusses maintenance requirements meant to protect your garden from severe insect or disease infestations. If you do get into trouble, the solutions probably will require time above and beyond regular maintenance.

How much time will tending the garden take? Professionals allow thirty minutes weekly to properly care for two or three large plants or four or five small plants. Of course, it doesn't take thirty minutes to dump a bucketful of water on each of three large plants, but that kind of handling doesn't promote a flourishing office garden either. Making sure the soil requires the amount of water you are about to dump on it is essential: Overwatering drowns plants. Pinching out tips to keep plants branching and removing dead leaves are aspects of plant care that are vital if you want a garden with which you'll be happy.

Along with the actual minutes that should be invested weekly in an office garden, there is the matter of regularity to consider. In the basement cloakroom of my church, a lovely row of hard-to-kill pothos was destroyed with great regularity until finally we put up a sign that read, PLEASE DO NOT WATER THE PLANTS, EVEN IF THEY NEED IT.

Someone regularly—not several someones erratically—must be responsible for maintenance. Before you install an ambitious office garden, do some collective soul-searching: Is there someone in your office (you, maybe) who loves to fuss over plants and whose boss (or maybe you're the boss) won't begrudge the time spent? If the answer is yes, then go ahead and load up with greens! Or, can you afford professional maintenance?

If there's no one around who is going to be responsible for the plants, best rethink your ambitions. You'll be happier with a few flourishing plants in your own corner or a mini-garden in your office than you will be with a languishing landscape spread over a large area.

Getting the Job Done

Obviously you can make an office garden, since a garden can be three plants on a windowsill or even one on a desk corner. However, if you want to create a garden the whole office will share, a little professional help will go a long way toward making a sounder and more effective garden. If management will give you any kind of budget for the project, accept it graciously and turn to Chapter 8 to see how to use your budget wisely.

If management can't help, try to raise the small fee needed to pay for a consultation with a professional, see Chapter 7 for design ideas, and read this book carefully from end to end.

If management wants to spend anything over $200 on the purchase of plants and make you responsible for design, purchase, and care, say "No, thank you." You or management could have a nervous breakdown at the first sign of a yellowing leaf.

There are too many variables in gardening, indoors and out, to make accepting the responsibility for a big expenditure comfortable, unless you are a professional. Accepting responsibility for the maintenance of an office garden makes sense if you enjoy plants. But I would think long and hard before saying yes to the responsibility for design and purchase. Professionals don't charge all that much for design, and only a small percentage of the purchase cost of the plants is added to the bill for time spent on purchase and installation. The few dollars the company will spend hiring a professional to design the garden are well worth it when your future peace of mind is at stake.

Putting Plants to Work

In New York these days, the windows of the big glass-sheathed skyscrapers are faced with leaves—trees, shrubs, hanging baskets, flowers, vines—all reaching for the sun. In the canyons of Wall Street, the little carts that used to sell hamburgers and hot dogs are selling live plants.

Behind today's explosion of plants on the work scene is the realization by more people that plants at work make you feel good and the discovery by management that there are economic and psychological benefits in putting plants to work.

Hubert A. Humphrey and Karl Menninger, for instance, are on record with statements backing the National Council for Therapy and Rehabilitation through Horticulture. Why?

Roger Carroll, consulting architect for the Port Authority of New York and New Jersey, explains the effect of plants this way: "People relate to plants in a way they don't relate to man-made materials. People relating to plants relate to each other."

When Mr. Carroll designed plants into a Port Authority office installation in 1966, he suggested staffers adopt a protective attitude toward any bugs that might turn up. "Knit little leads and leashes—think of them as pets." He got a lot of laughs. "Having something to share smiles over—that's one way plants humanize and relax the atmosphere at work."

Plants used as dividers and for screening also equalize privileges within offices. In the traditional office, windows to see through and sills to grow plants on belong to the privileged. The big central bull-pen section belongs to the have-nots. By using plants instead of walls as dividers in the central section, the have-nots are given views and plants of their own.

Industrial psychologist Lawrence Zeitlin, of the City University of New York, sees in the use of plants economic and physiological as well as psychological benefits: "You can house 25 to 30 percent more workers at a lower cost per person by using plants for partitioning. If the need is for flexible partitions, plants are even more of an economy. [It] costs less to move plants than walls."

Plants also improve the air, add pleasant amounts of humidity during the too-dry heating season, and make good sound barriers and absorbers.

Mr. Zeitlin sees the Ford Foundation in midtown New York and the Bell Laboratories in Holmdel, New Jersey, as buildings that make clear the profound psychological benefits plants bring to work complexes. "These futuristic structures use interior gardens to create a harmonious balance between the future and the past."

Mr. Zeitlin's theory is that when forests threatened the civilization we were carving from wilderness, cities seemed the good, peaceful, safe places. "Now that noisy, stressful urban centers are focusing our lives, the forests seem to be symbols of lost innocence and purity. The presence of plants creates a balance between organic and nonorganic life that is reassuring and relaxing."

Earl Hubbard, futurist and space philosopher, author of *Our Need for New Worlds*, has yet another view. He goes through the looking glass of time and comes out on the side where our moon and the planets are colonies of earth: "Environments there will likely be enclosed as are our most futuristic work complexes today. In meeting the basic human needs created by today's structures, we are evolving the large-scale terrariums that could house us on extraterrestrial worlds."

Studies are in progress seeking concrete scientific data on the effect of plants on sensitive technological equipment and on hospital patients, as well as in work situations and shopping malls. In time, the executive in charge of decorating the work scene will have exact information on the effects of plants in closed environments, terranean or lunar. For now, we can sum up the major benefits of office gardens this way: Plants at work make people happy. Happiness is of concrete value, and no one knows it better than the management of a happy staff.

2
Little Plants at Work

At work, small plants usually are personal plants—the miniature *Begonia rex* whose exquisite coloring you've nurtured in a bit of light from a sunny window and the baby aloe you are growing on a neighbor's sill. But a lot more can be done with the small plants than you might think. Before we go into that, let me say that you can grow small plants in lighting you may previously have considered useless.

Growing

A lot of the small plants described on the following pages will do well in the light of a desk lamp that has an ordinary incandescent bulb. Even African violets (*Saintpaulia*, page 162) have adapted and bloomed in lamplight burned about 12 hours a day. If your light can't be on that long, you may get permission to burn it into the night; an inexpensive timer ($8 or more) makes turning it on or off in your absence possible.

1 *Begonia rex* 'Merry Christmas'; **2** *Begonia masoniana*; **3** *Chlorophytum comosum*; **4** *Cyrtomium falcatum*; **5** *Aloe variegata*; **6** *Peperomia sandersii*; **7** *Maranta leuconeura massangeana*; **8** *Polyscias balfouriana marginata*

Under my friend's desk light a white-flowered *Oxalis regnellii* has bloomed and so have many of his small gloxinias (see Chapter 6, page 156). Bird's-nest sansevierias, rooted cuttings of Chinese evergreen, small-leafed English ivies (*Hedera helix*, page 131), the marantas, calathea, are a few of the small plants he has grown under a desk lamp.

I haven't tried every small plant in this chapter under a desk lamp, but enough have succeeded so that I feel safe in suggesting that you can try almost any small plant that interests you under an ordinary lamp. But use your head. Don't try those plants noted for their need for many hours of direct sunlight daily—miniature roses, for instance. Try plants with lesser light needs; they are almost sure to succeed.

Ordinary (incandescent) bulbs give off more heat than the fluorescents, so you must place plants a safe distance from the bulb. How do you test? The same way you test water for heat—use your hand. Place your hand at leaf level for a minute or so. A gentle glow won't hurt your plants; heat high enough to make your hand uncomfortable after a few minutes may be too much for the plant. The most practical spotlight for a desk plant is one on an extendable base: This lets you raise and lower it until the heat reaching the surface at the top leaves is minimal.

You must also place the plants under enough light to meet their light requirements. If the plant requires lots of light, try a 75-watt bulb (or two 60-watt bulbs) set as close to the plant as you can place it without overheating the leaves. Expect to make adjustments over the first several weeks, and keep close track of what is happening to the plant. If the leaves begin to show browned areas in a few days, the light is too close or too strong or you are burning the lights for too long a period. If the leaves are becoming pale, the stems spindly, or if new leaves are appearing farther and farther apart on the stems, the plant is short of light. Lower the bulb or increase the wattage or the length of time the lamp is on daily.

What about desks without lamps? All desks have enough light to read by, or you wouldn't be working there. Many of the plants in this chapter, in this book for that matter, have been grown in light from overhead office fluorescents.* If the fluores-

---

* We assume that the height of the average office ceiling is 8 feet.

cents are directly over your desk, you should be able to grow almost any of the plants. If the fluorescents are to one side, you may need to augment the light with a desk lamp. On the other hand, enough additional light may be reaching your desk from nearby windows to keep the plants happy.

Whatever the setup, you're going to have to experiment until you find the right light combination, for plant needs vary, not only from species to species, but from specimen to specimen as well. You will note that sometimes in the descriptions of maintenance requirements given in this book specific wattage has been given. These are conditions that have worked for me and might work for you. Then again, they might not. Once more I emphasize the need for experimentation and patience.

Plants take time to adjust to new situations. Give them time. Don't suppose that one browned leaf means disaster or that the plant can't adapt to the position in which you have placed it. The plants described here are tough—adaptable is what I really mean. Have faith.

Decorating

Now, back to what you can do with small plants. A little plant alone can warm your heart but won't make much of a splash in terms of design. But repeat the leaf pattern in several pots—some elevated on plastic cubes to make a miniature terrace garden—and you have a really exciting garden.

If you find the repetition of one leaf pattern boring, then group several different varieties of the same species. In groups of this kind, all the pots have similar light needs and watering patterns. This makes maintenance easy and pretty foolproof. Species and varieties with similar needs can be planted together in one big, beautiful dish garden (see Chapter 7).

Another exciting way to use small plants is to put together two or three small ones of contrasting foliage types with a single flowering plant, a miniature African violet, for instance, or a colorful variegated plant, such as coleus or a *Begonia rex*, miniature or baby.

Small plants, alone or in groups, charm bare spaces on desks, on worktables, and on coffee tables, sills, and the tops of heat

Hedera helix: **1** variegated leaf; **2** plain leaf

convectors below sills or against a wall. Won't heat or air conditioning harm plants? Yes—blasts of heat in particular harm many plants. And I've cooked enough plants to death by failing to move them from the top of a heating unit after the heat came on in October to be wary of such locations. However, you can convert a heat-convector surface into a mini-greenhouse, and Chapter 7 describes how.

Another area in which small plants are effective and thrive is the washroom. Is there anything more barren than the average washroom? It's cold as clean ice and illuminated by brilliant overheads—sterile as a hospital operating room. But washroom lights are intensified by white walls and mirrors, and this combination is first class for many of the plants listed here, big and small. A stepped plant holder displaying half a dozen cascading fuzzy little ferns would do wonders for most washrooms I've seen; so would just a few wandering jew (*Tradescantia*) cuttings grouped on the countertops, on glass shelves above the countertops, or on the vanity ledge under a mirror.

A bookcase is another good place for the display of small plants, especially if there's a little window light reaching it. If you can spare a shelf or a portion of a shelf, you can install grow lights on the underside of the shelf above and place trays filled with moist pebbles beneath on which you can grow a whole dramatic garden of small plants. The same concept can be used to create a wall garden. Just stack shelves, each with its own set of lights hidden by a narrow valance. This is a terrific way to landscape a dark corner of a reception area—or any other spot of gloom. Tier on tier of lights with bright-leaved coleus or miniature rex begonias cheers the heart of the crossest of office grumps. This setup, along with the bookcase garden, is described in detail in Chapter 7.

Back to singleton plants: When there's going to be room only for one, choose a plant that is unusual—the jade plant (*Crassula argentea*, pages 38–39), or the mistletoe fig (*Ficus lyrata*, page 80), for instance—and dramatize it with a spotlight. Or, if the space is large and uncrowded, choose a big-leafed plant like Chinese evergreen (*Aglaonema*, page 26) or one that is bold and colorful, like cathedral windows (*Calathea*, page 35).

Watering

Always use tepid water!

Really small plants, the miniatures, are usually happy in pots 2 to 4 inches in diameter (across the top). The pots may be as deep as they are wide or shallower, and they do not have much

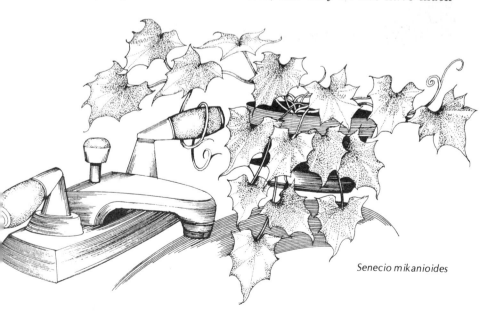

Senecio mikanioides

soil in them. The message is this: They dry out quickly and need watering often. Sometimes, on a dry, breezy summer day or at the peak of the winter heating season, a 2-inch pot may dry out a few hours after you water it and need watering again before you leave for home.

Pots 3, 4, and 5 inches across usually need watering every three or four days, but that varies depending on office conditions. When you acquire a new small plant, check the pot every day for a few weeks, so you can water as needed. After a month or so, you will discover the right watering pattern for the new plant and can then plan a schedule.

One way to improve the health of small plants and cut down on watering is to group several plants in a large saucer that has been filled with small river-washed pebbles. Keep the pebbles moist by filling the tray when it dries out, but add only enough water to bring the level to just below, not touching, the pot bottoms. Plants are healthiest when there is good air circulation in the pots, and to get an air flow, it must be possible for the bottom of the pots to breathe. They can't when they are sitting in water.

Feeding

Most plant-food containers direct you to dilute the contents and give indications for frequency of feeding. When you are dealing with office plants, a good general rule is to feed half as much as directed or even less. You don't want the plants to grow significantly; you just want them to have enough food to stay healthy. (Remember, after all, that while at home an overgrown plant can always be moved to a larger space or a different room, office space is usually limited, and while plants can work to motivate you, claustrophobia, at the same time, can be a hazard!)

Putting plant food into their water isn't the only way to feed plants. Every 6 to 12 months (6 months or less for very small plants) its a good idea to repot in fresh soil. Unless they are one of the few species that hate transplanting (these are noted in text), repotting is one of the best ways to keep your office garden flourishing. Old soil builds up acids and fallout from plant foods. Changing the soil gives plants a fresh start, and they usually show it. Chapter 8 describes repotting in detail.

Containers

When you have lots of small plants grouped on a desk or file cabinet, water marks on the surfaces are likely accidents. One way to avoid the problem is to group the plants on a single large plastic saucer or tray filled with pebbles and backed with felt. Another way out is to provide cachepots for each small pot. A cachepot (a French word whose literal translation is "hide-pot") is a plant container without a drainage hole.

Choose ceramic saucers carefully. They're pretty, but the unglazed kind hold moisture that eventually stains wood. Some of the glazed types have unglazed bottoms. Glaze them yourself by painting them with polyurethane. Or, if they're tiny, paint them with clear nail polish—several coats will waterproof them. After the last coat, stick on a felt circle the size of the saucer bottom. It will protect the desk from scratches as well as water marks.

If you do spill water on a desk top, wipe it dry at once; usually it won't spot. If you miss a puddle on a polished wooden surface and find a stain a few hours later, don't panic. If you don't wax over it for several days, it usually will go away or become almost unnoticeable.

If the stain remains—a pale ghost on the gleaming surface—try rubbing it with a mixture of linseed oil (I have used plain vegetable oil on occasion) and cigarette ash. That may be enough to remove the marred top coat of varnish. Or, rub very gently with double 00 steel wool dipped in colored furniture polish. When it dries, polish carefully with a heavily colored furniture oil.

Selection

If you buy a small plant just because you fell in love with it at the plant shop, your pleasure may be short-lived. The plant may hate its location or outgrow it in a few months.

To buy the right plant for the location you have in mind, you should know the plant's needs and capabilities. You might find it handy to take this book with you any time you are going to expose yourself to the appeal of a shopful of growing green things. Then you can look up the plant you're tempted to buy and judge whether it will work out in the spot you have in mind. The plants here are listed alphabetically by their horticultural names. The common names appear alphabetically in the Index.

One major consideration when you buy a plant is what it will look like when it grows up—or whether it will grow up at all. Small plants may be naturally small and never grow much more than 4 or 6 inches tall. Or, they may be low growers—to 12 inches high. Still others may be slow growers that will stay at around 8 or 12 inches for ages but will eventually grow into trees or shrubs. Or they may be babies of fast growers that will have outgrown the place you have for small plants in a few months. The only way you can tell—other than asking the salesperson, who often cannot answer your questions—is to look up the information.

On the pages that follow, I've listed the best of the small plants for offices and noted their peculiarities: their sizes at maturity, their needs for light, temperature, water, food, grooming, and so on. These are the small plants most professional landscapers use as desk plants in the temperate areas of the country.

In California you'll find babies of some plants temperate-zone nurseries sell only as larger plants. Among them and described in Chapter 5 are *Cissus*, which is grape ivy, *Scindapsus aureus* (pothos), *Syngonium podophyllum* (nephthytis), *Philodendron cordatum* or *P. oxycardium*. In Chapter 4 you'll find *Brassaia actinophylla* (schefflera), *Chamaedorea erumpens* (bamboo palm), and *Howeia fosteriana* (kentia palm). If you can locate young plants of these in your area, they make lovely desk plants for a time and need relatively little light. The instructions for handling these plants when they are mature apply to the baby sizes as well, except you'll have to water the younger ones more often than instructions for mature plants suggest.

There are other lovely small plants not listed here because they are either hard to find or hard to handle, but they are worth a try once your basic garden is thriving: *Ctenanthe*, *Pedilanthus*, small *Malpighia*, small *Sedum morganianum*, *Rhipsalis*, and *Pellaea rotundifolia* are some of the prettiest.

The Plants

Agave Species

RESUMÉ: The agaves are wonderfully easy, slow-growing plants from the desert. Symmetrically spaced pointed leaves make them look like prickly rosettes. The best known is a biggy—the century plant. It reaches to about 10 feet indoors (40 feet in the desert). Most often you see small species and babies planted with cacti in dish-sized desertscapes. Suppliers usually carry *Agave filifera* and *A. victoria-reginae*. After many years, these will grow to a few feet and produce flowers occasionally. *A. filifera* has bright green leaves with white edges, 8 to 10 inches long; curled filaments grow along the edges. *A. victoria-reginae* has dark green leaves with gray along the edges. *A. stricta*, called the hedgehog agave, is less easy to find but a very good, stable office worker, an ideal choice if you doubt your talent as a plant parent.

RELOCATION: Because they grow very slowly indeed, agaves make great small plants for a sunny desk or table corner. When bigger, they can be used as accents in groups of plants on top of sunny file cabinets or in windows with a southern exposure.

SITUATIONS WANTED: Agaves are especially tolerant of high heat and dry air. They have problems when temperatures fall below 55 degrees. They'll adapt to direct sun in an east or west window, but the ideal is a south window. They also adapt to strong fluorescent light. You can also experiment by placing them 3 inches below the tubes or under a 75-watt or two 60-watt desk lamps. The latter has worked for me.

SALARY REQUIREMENTS: In spring and summer, water agaves weekly. The rest of the year, water only when the surface soil feels really dry. Feed a diluted solution of all-purpose plant food every two weeks in spring and summer. Feed half as much the rest of the year. When the plant outgrows its pot, repot in a cactus-soil mixture. Be sure to supply good drainage by placing an inch or two of pebbles in the pot before adding the soil.

FYI: A combination of wet soil and cold air will rot the roots and kill the plant.

Aglaonema Species
CHINESE EVERGREEN

RESUMÉ: The Chinese evergreens are graceful slow-growing foliage plants from Asia and Africa. Most get to be 24 inches tall and have narrow leaves 6 to 12 inches long. They are usually offered in sizes about 12 inches tall, in pots 8 inches across the top. In about two years, they'll grow to mature height—18 inches. *Aglaonema modestum* is the one correctly called Chinese evergreen, but suppliers tend to apply the name to all species. 'Silver King' is a beautiful silver-gray hybrid worth searching out. Most other species are bright green with splotches and splashes of white or silver.

RELOCATION: A Chinese evergreen is a double investment: a desk plant for now, eventually a small shrub. Even on young plants, the leaves are big enough to make some impact when seen on file cabinets across a large room. As your aglaonema reaches mature size, place it on a stand to create the effect of a small shrub.

SITUATIONS WANTED: Indoor office lighting is fine. It can be from fluorescents, or it can be from regular incandescent lights, as long as the light is bright enough to read by. That's all that aglaonemas need. (Light reaching the floor *directly below* a window is less than the light that reaches the floor several feet from a window, because of the sill's shadow.) Avoid placing an aglaonema near hot or cold drafts. Temperatures of 72 degrees days and as low as 55 nights are fine.

SALARY REQUIREMENTS: Aglaonemas prefer evenly moist soil but won't drop dead if they dry out occasionally. When you first get your plant, check it Mondays and Thursdays and water the soil if it is less than moist on the surface. Feed all-purpose plant food half as often as suggested on the container but feed it year round. Plan to repot annually in fresh all-purpose soil. Pour water through the soil every few months to clear out accumulated fertilizer salts.

FYI: Cold drafts spoil the plant.

Aloe Species
UNGUENTINE PLANT

RESUMÉ: The aloes are slow growers from desert areas, as are the agaves, which they resemble. They're succulents with stiff, pointed leaves that grow symmetrically around a stem. *Aloe vera* is the only one whose common name is unguentine plant (pulp from it heals burns), but that name is commonly used for all the aloes. *A. vera* is a rather large plant and makes a striking indoor shrub, but there are smaller species, such as *A. aristata*, about 6 inches tall, that make good desk plants. In bright light, the aloe will produce orange-red blooms in midwinter.

RELOCATION: The tiny aloes are great in desertscape dish gardens or alone in bright little ceramic or plastic pots. A collection makes a good windowsill garden for a south exposure.

SITUATIONS WANTED: As long as there is lots of sun, the aloes will do very well. They're tolerant of high heats and dry air. Temperatures cannot fall below 55 degrees without causing problems, but they can range up into the high 70s. The ideal location is a sunny south, east, or west window. However, when young, aloes will acclimatize to a very bright north window, especially if there are white walls or mirrors nearby to reflect all the available light. Try miniatures and young plants close to the tubes in a fluorescent garden or under a strong desk lamp; they should adapt. If at any time you move this plant outdoors after a winter indoors, do so gradually; a sudden change from low light to direct summer sun can burn the leaves.

SALARY REQUIREMENTS: Water when the surface feels dry— probably weekly in the spring and summer months. Water well enough so that water seeps into the saucer. An hour later pour off excess. Feed diluted solutions of all-purpose plant food all year round, half as often as the directions suggest. Repot, if needed, in fresh cactus soil with an inch or two of pebbles in the bottom for drainage.

FYI: Badly drained soil that leaves the plant soaking wet for days will rot the roots.

Ardisia Crispa
CORALBERRY

RESUMÉ: This tropical begins as a desk plant with shiny ever-green leaves and in a few or several years will grow into a 4-foot tree. It is quite beautiful. Mature, it produces clusters of small fragrant pink or white flowers in spring and summer. These turn to bright coral-colored berries in fall and last through winter. Most suppliers carry it in desk size; it's rare to find a mature specimen for sale. Though the correct name is *Ardisia crispa*, sometimes it is called A. crenulata.

RELOCATION: Use it alone on a big desk or in the center of a large table, on a large sill, or on a filing cabinet. It is graceful as part of a group of plants and makes a nice contrast for feathery small foliage plants in paler shades of green. When it reaches tree size, you can feature it against a blank wall on a low pedestal. Once it begins to produce berries, it is twice as effective, either as part of a grouping of foliage plants or alone. It's a good choice for a well-lighted washroom since it needs humidity.

SITUATIONS WANTED: Give coralberry good light, moderate warmth, plenty of humidity, and the plant is easy to grow. Any bright light will do, but avoid direct sunlight in summer. It will succeed directly under overhead fluorescents and should do well under a strong spotlight. Temperatures of 70 degrees during the day are best, though it will take higher temperatures. Low at night can be to 55 degrees.

SALARY REQUIREMENTS: The soil must be kept evenly moist; if it gets bone-dry, the plant will suffer. Test the soil of the desk-size plant every three days and water if it feels dry. Daily misting is beneficial. Repot annually—every six months if you're eager for a tree-size plant—in a half-and-half mixture of all-purpose potting soil and humus. Feed all-purpose plant food in fall and winter; feed blooming-type plant food in spring and summer; every two weeks should be sufficient year round. If you are eager for the plant to grow from desk size to tree size, feed as often as the fertilizer directions suggest.

FYI: Red spider mites attack when air is hot and stale. Daily misting and evenly moist soil help keep them away.

Aspidistra elatior
CAST-IRON PLANT

RESUMÉ: Lots prettier than the name suggests, this is a handsome foliage plant 12 to 24 inches high with big, 2-foot-long leaves in dark green or green striped with white. The striped kind is *Aspidistra elatior variegata*. There is also a dwarf with white-spotted leaves. The aspidistra flourished in cool, dim Victorian parlors and is just about indestructible. These days it is often snubbed, because the dim corners in which it usually gets stuck don't show off its assets. Also it is very slow growing, and since it needs and gets little attention, the leaves collect dust, and it begins to look like a stiff plastic plant. Nevertheless, it is one of the best plants you can buy for work, especially if you're neglectful. The dwarf variety is great on desks.

RELOCATION: This is an effective foliage plant anywhere, especially if it gets good care. The standard size is large for a desk but makes a handsome accent on top of a filing cabinet, raised on a low pedestal in a corner of a small office, or centered on big work tables. The dwarf size is great in a desk group with ferns. Several grown together make a pretty dish garden.

SITUATIONS WANTED: The aspidistra grows in light bright enough to read by, either from a bright north window or back from an east or west window, or under fluorescents. It responds to temperatures between 50 and 70 degrees. It will do poorly in heat. A good choice for a cool corner.

SALARY REQUIREMENTS: Weekly watering—enough to keep the soil evenly moist—is all that's needed. If the plant dries out, it will recover once watered and should show little browning of the leaf edges. Mist often if temperatures are over 70 degrees. Feed all-purpose plant food about half as often as directed on the container. The leaves grow very little in any season, so feeding should be light. Using all-purpose potting soil, repot yearly to keep the plant flourishing. Dust the leaves regularly to keep them pretty, and wash occasionally with a wet cloth if they need it.

FYI: You can kill an aspidistra by combining bone-dry soil and temperatures over 75 degrees.

Asplenium nidus
BIRD'S-NEST FERN

RESUMÉ: Bird's-nest fern looks more like a big-leafed foliage plant than like the plants we usually call ferns. It is one of the most beautiful and interesting indoor plants. It has handsome leathery green leaves that can be as long as 2 feet and as much as 10 inches wide. The height of the plants at maturity is usually about 2 feet. The leaves grow from a central cone, rosette fashion, and have a dark spine and wavy margins. The common name, bird's-nest fern, refers to the brown central cone from which the leaves sprout. At certain seasons, spores (which are the fern's equivalent of seeds) cluster in neat rows on the underside of mature leaves. Don't mistake them for some awful infestation from Mars—they're pretty!

RELOCATION: A mature bird's-nest fern is a handsome, relatively large desk plant and an attention getter used alone. A row of planters filled with bird's-nest ferns makes a great office divider. Or you can use one to three on top of a filing cabinet or on a large worktable.

SITUATIONS WANTED: Bird's-nest fern flourishes in bright light of any sort and does not need direct sun. Young ferns will grow well under fluorescent lights, and mature plants acclimatized to this kind of light do very well in most office lighting. Hot stale air and blasts of hot air wither old growth and prevent new growth from developing. Ferns are most successful in temperatures ranging between 60 and 70 degrees but suffer below 55 degrees. Fresh air and humidity are important to this variety and the other ferns.

SALARY REQUIREMENTS: Add enough water once or twice weekly to keep the soil evenly moist. Air the room daily, too, if you can. Wipe the plant with a wet cloth weekly or monthly. Feed all-purpose plant food about a third as often as package directs. Repot annually in a mixture of three parts African violet or terrarium soil and one part sphagnum moss.

FYI: Occasionally brown scale attacks bird's-nest ferns. (Don't mistake the spores described above for scale.)

Beaucarnea recurvata
PONYTAIL
ELEPHANT FOOT

RESUMÉ: Beaucarnea is a desert plant whose leaves look a little like a fountain. The long narrow leaves grow upward in a tuft and then fall over gracefully. In mature plants, the leaves can be 6 feet long. Grown indoors in pots, the beaucarneas get to be about 6 feet tall and about 2 feet across—very elegant and quite striking. The stem that produces this fountain of foliage looks like a long-necked jug. Actually, it's a moisture reservoir and one reason the plant can take a lot of neglect. Suppliers usually offer desk sizes 12 to 24 inches high.

RELOCATION: The smaller-size beaucarneas are graceful table or sill plants. They're on the tall side—nothing to cuddle under a desk lamp. Because the fountaining foliage is so distinct in young and old plants, beaucarneas demand a spotlight and a place all their own.

SITUATIONS WANTED: Light needs are variable. Instructions usually call for full sun in an east, west, or south window; however, a tree-size beaucarnea I know is placed in summer under taller trees in light comparable to that from a brightly lit west-facing window. Beaucarnea should do well, once acclimatized, under strong fluorescents. Or try it under a single strong spotlight. Temperatures are okay up to 75 degrees but not under 50 degrees.

SALARY REQUIREMENTS: Water well but only after the surface has dried. Remember: It's storing a supply of moisture in its bulbous base. Feed all-purpose plant food year round, half as often as suggested on food containers. Repot once a year or when the plant has outgrown its present container. Use three parts all-purpose potting soil with one part sand. Wipe the leaves gently (they can split easily) with a damp cloth every month or two.

FYI: Water left standing in the saucer can cause problems and so can soil that holds too much water, so be sure to add extra sand if you repot and put an inch or two of pebbles for drainage in the bottom of the pot.

Begonia rex
REX BEGONIA

RESUMÉ: The rex begonias are grown for the beauty of their textured, colorful foliage. They are forms of *Begonia rexii* (pronounced *rex-ee-eye*, with the accent on the *eye*). Among striking varieties is 'Helen Teupel,' a bushy plant with sharply lobed long leaves, dark fuchsia red along the center and margins, metallic green along the veins, with silvery-pink areas in between. In 'Merry Christmas,' the center is a velvety blood red edged by silver and pink; the outer zone is nile green, edged with fuchsia red. The iron cross begonia, *B. masoniana* (not a real rex) is blue green with a dark red-brown Maltese cross in the center. Young plants and miniatures are 6 to 10 inches tall; at maturity standard-size plants are about 18 to 24 inches tall.

RELOCATION: Use babies and miniatures, singly or in pairs, on your desk; mature standard sizes work well on big tables or grouped in planters on file cabinets or atop room dividers. The showiest varieties are good color accents for groups of green foliage plants. Combine begonia varieties with contrasting foliage for a truly colorful display in any size.

SITUATIONS WANTED: Humidity and warmth (65 to 75 degrees) are essential. Avoid hot or cold drafts. Rexes grow well under fluorescent lights or in direct light from a bright window. Two 60-watt bulbs burned eight hours daily have worked well for me.

SALARY REQUIREMENTS: Rex begonias must be kept evenly moist but never soggy, so check them twice weekly. If you are growing miniatures, group several in one big dish garden: You may have to water them twice daily in hot weather. You may like a group of small pots on a tray filled with moist pebbles. Mist daily or at least weekly. Feed all-purpose plant food about half as often as the container suggests. In late fall your plants may lose some leaves: Keep them drier during winter and withhold fertilizer until early spring. Repot as needed, or annually, in African violet or terrarium soil with pebbles in the pot bottom for good drainage.

FYI: Soggy soil combined with cold temperatures can kill rexes, especially if they are in drafty spots.

Cacti and Other Succulents

RESUMÉ: There are so many kinds of cacti and succulents in circulation it would take a book to name them. Succulents and cacti overlap; both grow in deserts and in jungles and are storers of water. They're thick-fleshed plants built to withstand droughts. (Pencil euphorbia, described on pages 44–45, is a typical succulent.) *Mammillaria*, which grows as a columnar cluster covered with prickles; *Cereus*, the tall, prickly, four-sided column; *Cephalocereus senilis*, the funny old-man cactus covered with silky white hair; and the prickly pear cactus, *Opuntia*, are among the most familiar cacti. *Lobivia, Mammillaria, Notocactus ottonis, N. rutilans*, and *N. haselbergii* are among easy-to-find cacti that bloom; however, you can't be sure of blooming unless you can provide them with a cool winter period of several months at 50 to 60 degrees. In tiny sizes, cacti are inexpensive. In sizes several feet tall, they cost a fortune—justifiably so, since they take years to grow. The babies are ideal desk and windowsill plants for neglectful, absent-minded, or traveling office gardeners as well as for those too-hot, too-sunny offices.

RELOCATION: A sunny windowsill or desk corner is a great place to display a dish desert garden or a collection of baby cacti in bright little plastic pots. Raise them on small square pedestals in colors that contrast with the pots.

Mammillaria elongata

1 *Opuntina;* **2** *Lobivia aurea*

SITUATIONS WANTED: Ideal light is provided in a south window or in a southeast or southwest window that gets many hours of sun daily. Best temperatures are 70 to 75 degrees, though cacti can take higher temperatures with equanimity, with lows at night to 55 degrees.

SALARY REQUIREMENTS: Though cacti can stand neglect, they'll grow fast if watered and fed regularly. Repot new purchases in generous-size pots filled with cactus soil; they're often sold in cramped pots and poor soil. Let surface soil dry completely before watering; never let cacti sit in saucer puddles. Feed all-purpose plant food during spring and summer only. If cooling cacti for bloom as described above, cut watering in half.

FYI: Black thrips and red spider mites may cause sunken, discolored areas.

Calathea makoyana
CATHEDRAL WINDOWS

RÉSUMÉ: Rather like a big prayer plant, cathedral windows makes a colorful potful, 18 to 20 inches tall and 24 or more inches wide. The oblong, olive-green leaves are patterned with darker green, and beneath that there's red in a delicate network of veins. In some varieties, the undersides of the leaves are maroon or burgundy red, and the surfaces are splotched, spotted, or veined in red. Calatheas are a better choice than prayer plant (*Maranta*) for an office if maintenance is going to be intermittent and haphazard.

RELOCATION: Small-size plants are nice combined in a big shallow dish with a dwarf palm (page 83), pothos (page 135), and hoya (page 132). These all respond to similar climate and treatment. In larger sizes, your desk will need only one. Two or three mature calatheas grouped on top of a file cabinet make a nice display. The strong color makes mature calatheas effective in a well-lighted washroom, and they respond well to the humidity there.

SITUATIONS WANTED: These do well on fairly low light—light from a north window, for instance, or a few feet back from a sunny east or west window. Temperatures that make you comfortable are good for calathea—below 60 degrees won't do, nor will steady diets of 75-degree heat.

SALARY REQUIREMENTS: Keep the soil evenly moist. Check the plant Mondays and Thursdays or every three days, and water if the surface is beginning to feel dry. If the soil dries too much, the leaf tips will brown. Misting often helps to keep calathea fresh looking; mist weekly in summer and as often as you can in winter. Feed all-purpose plant food half as often as container directs, year round. Calatheas send up offsets, baby plants: You can remove and pot these at any season to double your holdings and to keep the pot from becoming too crowded. In any case, repot annually, and remove the offsets then. Use African violet or terrarium soil; it which holds moisture well.

FYI: Dry soil and overheated rooms (75 degrees and up) will turn the leaf tips brown. Crowded plants won't flourish, so plan to repot or remove offsets as needed.

Chlorophytum comosum
SPIDER PLANT
AIRPLANE PLANT

RESUMÉ: When young, the spider plant makes a tuft of tall, broad grassy leaves, some plain green, some white striped inside. As the plant grows, it sends out long slender stalks that arch gracefully downward. Some sport tiny white flowers, most eventually are tipped by small nests of leaves that are new plants. They're just fascinating to watch develop. You can cut off the little airborne plants and root them in water or plant them in soil, and they'll grow. The variety 'Mandaianum' has bright yellow stripes. 'Picturatum' has broader leaves and yellow stripes.

RELOCATION: A big spider plant (except *Chlorophytum bichetii*) makes a great hanging basket, but while still just a tuft of grassy green, it's a dish plant. When the first slender stems begin to arch upward, move the plant to a corner so there will be a place for the stems to dangle free. Spider plants are impressive enough when mature for a promotion to the executive suite.

SITUATIONS WANTED: Moderate light and temperatures are all the spider plant needs, and it is very adaptable. Young plants can be started under fluorescent lights and will continue to grow under them. I have a big plant doing beautifully in a spot where it gets a little east light in the morning and a little west light in the afternoon. A tall lamp stands near it, and evenings when I work late or toward the end of winter afternoons, it gets good light from two 75-watt bulbs. Temperatures below 55 degrees are damaging, as is hot, dry, stale air.

SALARY REQUIREMENTS: Keep the soil evenly moist; if you don't, the leaf edges will very quickly brown and spoil the looks of a beautiful plant. One thing about watering: The spider plant's leaves are bent up, like a folded grass blade, and curve down. If you pour water on the leaves, they'll pour it right onto the floor, so keep the watering spout close to the soil. Feed with all-purpose plant food as directed on the container. Repot annually or when the pot becomes crowded. Flush thoroughly every few months to wash out acid buildup.

FYI: Symptoms of acid buildup are new growth blackened or rotted. Work limestone into the soil—one tablespoon for big plants—or flush the soil with lots and lots of water.

Coleus Species

RESUMÉ: Of the foliage plants, few are as colorful, inexpensive, or easy to handle as coleus. There are endless combinations of magenta pink, burgundy red, maroon, cream, and green, all varieties of *Coleus blumei*, 1 to 3 feet tall. You can buy packets of mixed seeds and grow bushels of coleus just for the cost of the seeds, soil, and containers. *C. blumei verschaffeltii* is considered the most beautiful. It has large glowing crimson leaves with nile green borders and purple in the center. Creeping coleus (*C. rehneltianus*) are magnificent in hanging baskets but hard to find.

RELOCATION: Coleus is great as a small accent plant on a desk, in a washroom, or in a group of green foliage plants. But the most dramatic use of coleus is in masses. Half a dozen contrasting varieties on a file cabinet, a worktable, anywhere, bring a glow of color to any office. Try a planter with tall coleus in the center, young coleus in paler colors surrounding the tall plants, and cascades of variegated myrtle or creeping coleus at the edges.

SITUATIONS WANTED: Coleus succeeds in temperatures ranging between 55 and 75 degrees. It grows a few feet back from a sunny south window, in a sunny east or west window, or bright north window. It also does well under fluorescents if the lights burn 16 to 18 hours a day and is super under the broad-spectrum fluorescents called grow lights. With less light, colors will be paler and plants grow spindly.

SALARY REQUIREMENTS: Keep the soil very moist and mist often. Leaves wilt when soil dries but usually recover when well watered. Edges may brown a little. If a plant is severely damaged, cut it back. Keep flowering tops pinched. Feed all-purpose plant food weekly. In late winter, cut 6- to 8-inch tips from your coleus, root them in water, plant in all-purpose soil, several tips to each pot, and discard the parent plant; it becomes played out after a season or two.

FYI: Some people's coleuses have problems with mealybugs.

Crassula argentea
JADE PLANT

RESUMÉ: The jade plant is a good choice for overheated offices. It's from South Africa, a compact succulent with stiff jade-green leaves, and grows slowly to about 3 feet tall. In strong light, the jade plant leaves take on a coppery tint around the edges. In pale light the leaves are lighter in color. The common jade plant is offered by most suppliers. Fun to look for are 'Variegated Jade,' whose green and grayish leaves are variegated cream to orange yellow with an orange-red edge, and 'Dwarf Ruby.'

Crassula argentea

RELOCATION: Young jade looks marvelous in a shiny or matte finish ceramic container on a desk, in a bookcase, or alone on a small table. It is like a small sculpture. Mature plants make dramatic low shrubs, handsome alone or combined with any of the palms (see Chapter 3).

SITUATIONS WANTED: Jade plants are tolerant of many different light situations if allowed time to adapt. A sunny south, east, or west window is fine, but jade also succeeds in light from a bright north window or right under fluorescents. If the leaves become very pale and grow sparsely along the branches (contrast new growth with original growth), light is too low. Place it nearer sunlight or closer to fluorescents, or burn the fluorescents longer.

SALARY REQUIREMENTS: Jade plant comes potted in rather gritty soil that drains very well. The surface soil should be allowed to get rather dry between waterings. Soggy soil and temperatures below 55 degrees are its enemies. It's a good choice if you have an overheated office, because it seems to withstand with equanimity temperatures up to 80 degrees. Feed with all-purpose or cactus plant food half as often as the container directs; in winter feed half as often. Repot in cactus soil when roots become potbound.

FYI: If the plant is losing its crispness, you may be overwatering or underwatering. Chances are it's overwatering. Sometimes mealybugs attack the jade plant.

Cyperus alternifolius
UMBRELLA PLANT

RESUMÉ: Willowy stems, each topped by an umbrella of grassy leaves—that's the umbrella plant. It is a semiaquatic perennial plant from Africa—one of the very few semiaquatics we grow indoors. At maturity the species called *Cyperus alternifolius* is 2 to 4 feet tall and looks like a cluster of palms. There's a dwarf variety, *C. a. gracilis*, which is about 18 inches tall. There is also *C. diffusus*, which is quite a different species with much broader and coarser leaves, not nearly as graceful. Choose *C. a. gracilis* for your desk and *C. alternifolius* if you want the plant to grow big enough to use in a larger space. There is a variegated kind that's quite pretty, too.

RELOCATION: The small umbrella plant shows off very well when grouped with desk plants that have dense, coarse foliage, or in a water garden, as described in Chapter 7. Mature plants are super in indoor pools if you have one available. Or you can group them with big pots of small-leafed English ivy, miniature evergreens, and even, oddly, with cacti and succulents. It's also a good plant for the washroom area, where you can dribble water over the leaves often—that's good for it. A poor plant for places where there are blasts of hot, dry air.

SITUATIONS WANTED: Moderate light—a bright north window or a few feet back from an east or west window. Temperatures should be between 60 and 70 degrees since the plant suffers when temperatures are over 75 degrees and below 55 degrees. Hot, dry, stale air browns the leaf tips and spoils its looks.

SALARY REQUIREMENTS: The soil must be kept moist to wet. Mist as often as possible. Feed all-purpose plant food year round half as often as recommended by container instructions. Repot in March in three parts all-purpose soil with one part humus. If you've bought *C. alternifolius* (the larger plant), take 3-inch cuttings in spring and root them in soil kept very moist. That will make babies for desk use. Shower the plant monthly if that is practical.

FYI: Red spider mites are a problem when the air is too hot and too dry. Mist often.

Cyrtomium falcatum
HOLLY FERN

RESUMÉ: This long-lived fern has individual leaves—they look a little like holly leaves. The name is pronounced *sear-toh-mee-um*, with the accent on *toh*. It's a durable fern even when mistreated, and when things are good, it grows so bushy you'll be thrilled. The kind usually offered is a variety called *Cyrtomium falcatum* 'Rochefordianum,' which has leaves more noticeably cut out, or hollylike, than the original species. Desk-size plants in 3- to 4-inch pots have a few dark green fronds on wiry stems and grow fairly slowly to a height of 12 to 24 inches. The leaves are up to 30 inches long and 8 inches wide.

RELOCATION: Desk-size plants are great anywhere a low-light plant is needed. A crisp accent in the washroom on the edge of the sink or on a glass shelf above the sink, the stiff dark foliage makes it a good foil for softer ferns; they can be grouped in a big dish garden with other ferns since their needs are similar. Mature plants look great in planters and at the foot of trees in big tubs.

SITUATIONS WANTED: A few feet from an east or west window is good or in a bright north window. If you've only a south window, set holly fern several feet back from it. Baby holly ferns will do well under fluorescents or desk lamps, and once acclimatized, they should succeed there as mature plants. Over 70-degree temperatures may cause you trouble, unless you mist very often and can air the room occasionally. Between 60 and 70 degrees is ideal. Avoid locations where there are blasts of hot air, near heat convectors, for instance.

SALARY REQUIREMENTS: Keep the soil evenly moist. Mist daily or several times weekly. Shower new plants monthly. Feed with all-purpose plant food half as often as directed on container. Be very careful not to overfeed, especially in winter when there is no growth. Repot when the outside stems are crowding close to the pot edge. Use African violet or terrarium soil.

FYI: Drafts of hot air wither new growth and may kill old fronds. Cut away dead fronds and mist often.

Davallia Species
RABBIT'S-FOOT FERN

RESUMÉ: This fern seems so delicate that you wonder how it stands anything but the most perfect environment. However, it's among the easiest to grow of the ferns. The common name, rabbit's-foot, refers to the roots, which cover the soil and creep down the sides of hanging baskets. They're hairy and look a little like rabbit's feet, long and slender. *Davallia bullata mariesii* completely covers its container with feathery plumes. *D. fejeensis* is an extraordinarily delicate species with narrow triangular fronds about a foot long. *D. f. plumosa*, a dainty dwarf, is perhaps the best choice for your desk since its fronds are more durable.

RELOCATION: Any young davallia makes a charming desk plant and when grown up is perhaps the most beautiful of all basket plants. It looks super on a plant stand or in a group on a file cabinet. The dwarf, *D. f. plumosa*, is nice with a small umbrella plant (page 40) and *Pilea cadierei* (page 52). Davallias are good choices for washrooms, when light is good and misting often is easy.

SITUATIONS WANTED: This is a plant that likes low light outdoors and does very well indoors as long as you don't place it in hot, direct sunlight. A bright north window or a few feet back from a sunny east or west window are ideal, or place it to the side of or several feet back from a south window. Young plants adapt to fluorescent lights and manage under a regular desk lamp as well, as long as they don't get much heat from the bulb. Best temperatures for davallias—as for most ferns—are 60 to 70 degrees. They can stand up to 75-degree heat if the air is freshened often and kept moist. You'll have trouble below 55 degrees.

SALARY REQUIREMENTS: Soil for ferns must be kept evenly moist but never soaking wet. If it dries out, you'll lose lots of fronds in just hours. Daily misting helps and is essential if temperatures are over 70 degrees. Feed all-purpose plant food but half as often as directed on the food container. Repot as plants outgrow containers, using African violet or terrarium soil. You can start new plants by transplanting divisions of the parent plant.

FYI: Hot, dry air wrecks a fern.

Dracaena sanderiana

RESUMÉ: The slow-growing dracaenas range from plants 2 feet tall to tree size at maturity. The kind you probably know best is *Dracaena fragrans*, a tall plant that looks like a giant cornstalk with leathery leaves. *D. sanderiana*, one of the slowest growing, is sold for terrariums and in 3-inch pots. It has slender leaves, milky green striped white, which grow in a small rosette from a slender cane stem. So durable are the dracaenas that most owners find them boring and give them little coddling. Washed occasionally and treated well, the dracaenas grow into very handsome plants, and once they are growing successfully, they can become office shrubs.

RELOCATION: *D. sanderiana* stands out in a terrarium or dish garden. Or make a group combining a baby dracaena in a 3-inch pot with a young fern (page 42) and a small pilea (page 52); the fern needs cooler air than the dracaena, but the dracaena will adapt.

SITUATIONS WANTED: Good light in a north window or light near a sunny east or west window is fine, so are fluorescents, grow lights, and desk lamps. Temperatures can be anywhere between 60 and 80 degrees—as long as there is lots of moist air moving around the plant.

SALARY REQUIREMENTS: Keep the soil evenly moist but never soggy. *D. sanderiana* can't take standing in dried-out soil, especially if the air around is hot and dry—the leaf tips will brown and die. In very high heat, daily misting will keep dracaenas flourishing. Because the plant is slow growing, the broad leaves tend to collect dust; if you can, plan to wash the leaves monthly. The best plant food for dracaenas is all-purpose; feed half as often as package directs. The taller types of dracaenas, notably *D. fragrans*, often become bare stemmed at the bottom. Growers air-layer the top part, and once it has roots, discard the bare lower sections. You can pot 3-inch tip cuttings of smaller dracaenas if you want to multiply your assets.

FYI: Hot, dry air can brown leaf tips. This means dracaenas are poor choices for sills near heating units; blasts of hot air right over a heat convector can kill a dracaena.

Euphorbia Species

RÉSUMÉ: The name Euphorbia applies to a large species of varied plants, from the finicky poinsettias to succulents and cacti that tolerate, may even especially *like,* offices in which the atmosphere is uncontrollably hot in winter. These plants divide into two general groups: leafless and rather weird (or fascinating) plants like the pencil euphorbia (*Euphorbia tirucallii*), which reaches to 30 feet in its native Africa; and cactuslike types like the flowering crown of thorns, *E. milii.* 'Bojeri' (crown of thorns) is a dwarf of *E. milii* and usually produces red flowers with new growth. Another popular euphorbia for this category is the hatrack plant, *E. lactea.* This one grows rather quickly and gets to be 3 to 6 feet tall. In Vietnam it is called dragon bones. In India it is made into a hot jam and used medicinally for rheumatism. All the euphorbias contain milky juice that may lead to dermatitis and is considered poisonous.

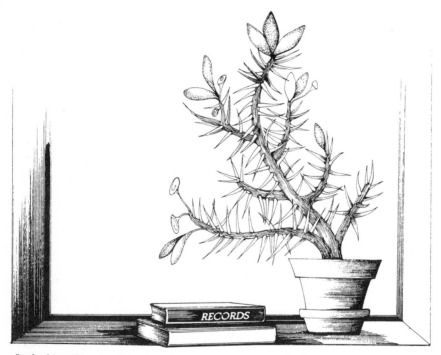

Euphorbia milii

RELOCATION: Euphorbias make an intriguing collection on a sunny sill. Maturing specimens, singly or grouped, make great accents on a table against any blank wall.

SITUATIONS WANTED: A sunny south window is best, though young plants may adapt to a sunny east or west window. You can grow mature plants for a time—say 3 or 4 months—under fluorescents or in a bright north window, but then they must have equal time in strong sunlight. 'Bojeri' grown in fluorescent light may acclimatize well enough to mature under fluorescents. The euphorbias will take a lot of hot, dry air.

SALARY REQUIREMENTS: When soil is dry, water from the top until the excess flows into the saucer. After an hour, empty the saucer. Feed nonflowering cacti and succulents all-purpose plant food; feed flowering types African violet plant food. If you break a section from a cactus, allow it to dry out overnight, then set the section to grow in cactus soil. If pots become crowded, repot succulents in all-purpose soil. Add two parts peat moss to three parts all-purpose soil for crown of thorns ('Bojeri').

FYI: Lack of light causes leaves to become pale and spindly. Mealybugs occasionally attack.

Ficus diversifolia
MISTLETOE FIG

RESUMÉ: The ficuses are variations on the fig tree. There's a big group that grows indoors, ranging in height from *Ficus pumila*, the tiny creeping fig (page 130), to trees such as *F. benjamina*, the lovely weeping fig (page 107). The India rubber plant, with its big rubbery leaves, is another member of this genus. *F. diversifolia* begins as a woody table or desk plant and grows to a small shrub size. Round leaves, speckled gray, and small yellow-gray nobs of fruit perpendicular to the main stem make it quite fascinating.

RELOCATION: Mistletoe fig stands out anywhere but doesn't look enough like mistletoe to do you any good at Christmas. It looks great on a big white sill in a north window, on a big table that stands against a bare wall, or against bare washroom tiles; or try it in a group with contrasting foliage, for instance a dish garden carpeted with *F. pumila*, creeping fig.

SITUATIONS WANTED: Bright light and moisture are important to all the ficuses. Bright light can be light near a sunny east or west window, a few feet back from a south window, or right in a north window. Ficuses also thrive directly under strong fluorescents, a fluorescent spot, or an incandescent floodlight. Temperatures between 55 and 75 degrees are okay, but mine have always done best in a cool bright room, around 68 degrees.

SALARY REQUIREMENTS: Water thoroughly, then don't water again until surface soil is dry. Pour water on till it seeps into the saucer, wait an hour, then pour off excess. Mist the leaves daily during the first months of the plant's adjustment to the office atmosphere and as often as possible thereafter. Feed all-purpose plant food half as often as package directs, year round. Repot in all-purpose soil in spring but only after the container has filled up with strong, healthy roots.

FYI: A ficus drops its leaves if the soil is too moist, too dry, or if there's not enough light. How to know which it is? Experiment. Be patient.

Ficuses also drop their leaves in the process of becoming accustomed to a new environment, and the plant may be okay where it is. The main thing is not to panic!

Fittonia verschaffeltii argyoneura
FITTONIA

RÉSUMÉ: The South American fittonias are dear little creepers with very showy leaves. The round, thin papery leaves of *Fittonia verschaffeltii argyoneura* are a strong green heavily and beautifully netted with white veins. There's another kind, *F. v. pearcei,* whose leaves are a lighter green netted with pink veins. These are perfect little desk plants because they grow in a very trim fashion without the constant pinching and pruning most creepers need to stay in shape. *F. v. argyoneura* needs 8 to 10 inches of pot space on which to spread out.

RELOCATION: The fittonias appear in most terrarium groupings, and here they thrive: They're high-humidity plants. A neat way to display a single plant is in a 10-inch-wide glass candy jar whose lid can be removed when there's lots of moisture in the air—summer, for instance, when windows are open. Or, set them under fluorescents in a big multi-plant office terrarium. Big terrariums are great for the reception area, too. If your fittonia thrives and grows out of bounds, try it in a small, moss-lined hanging basket under good light, but don't place the basket high because the air may be too dry.

SITUATIONS WANTED: Temperatures can range between 65 and 75 degrees, as long as the air is moist (30-percent moisture is ideal). Light can be from fluorescents, grow lights, spots and floods with incandescent bulbs, or just desk lamps. Fittonia can stand 2 or 3 hours of direct sun in an east or west window in winter. Avoid drafts, hot and cold.

SALARY REQUIREMENTS: Keep the soil evenly moist—that's the first requirement. The next is, be sure to empty the saucer one hour after watering. Feed diluted all-purpose plant food half as often as directed. Mist daily, unless fittonia is in a terrarium or covered dish. Repot annually in African violet or all-purpose soil. You can start baby plants in moist vermiculite just by rooting 3-inch tip cuttings at any season.

FYI: Poor drainage and hot or cold drafts can kill.

Maranta leuconeura
PRAYER PLANT
RABBIT TRACKS

RESUMÉ: These low-growing, lush tropicals have big leaves spotted or striped chocolate maroon to red and light green. The name prayer plant describes the way leaves fold together at night in pairs. *Maranta leuconeura kerchoviana*, called rabbit-tracks, is marked with irregular dabs of chocolate color evenly spaced along the sides; the chocolate turns pale green at maturity. A variation with green markings is 'Manda's Emerald.' *M. l. massangeana* is the kind called cathedral windows; this one has narrow red stripes arching out from a feathery center of silver, and looks like a bigger, coarser version of the prayer plant. Both varieties produce tiny flowers on long graceful stems.

RELOCATION: Though only a foot or so tall, the prayer plant's big leaves make it one of the largest desk plants. The spread at maturity is 18 inches across. Great for big worktables, end tables in the reception area, countertops, desk-high planters.

SITUATIONS WANTED: Fluorescents, a direct north window, or a few feet back from an east or west window are good spots. Temperatures to 70 or 72 degrees in the days and to 50 degrees at night are ideal.

SALARY REQUIREMENTS: Keep the soil evenly moist and mist often. A prayer plant is easy to grow, but the leaf edges brown easily if the plant dries. (Cut way the spoiled area with scissors. The rest of the leaf will eventually go but will be replaced by new growth.) If you can, shower monthly. Feed all-purpose plant food half as often as the container suggests. Repot in African violet or all-purpose soil when the container becomes crowded, or remove divisions and start new pots. Should your prayer plant seem to die, take it home and maintain it for several months. Sometimes they resurrect themselves.

FYI: Red spider attacks in hot dry air. Mist and shower more often until the infestation is under control.

Nephrolepis exaltata bostoniensis
BOSTON FERN

RESUMÉ: When you think fern, the kind you probably are seeing in your mind is a Boston fern. It's the one most often grown in indoor gardens, a reliable, graceful, fast-growing plant since Victorian days. There's a standard size whose fronds grow to 3 feet long, sometimes 5—a big imposing plant once mature. There's also a dwarf variety, *Nephrolepis exaltata bostoniensis compacta*, which is better for desk or tabletops. If your office does well with Boston fern, you should try the perfectly gorgeous 'Fluffy Ruffles,' another dwarf of *N. exaltata*.

RELOCATION: Babies of either the dwarf or the standard-size Boston fern have a rather large wingspread and need room to arch downward. Place young plants either on a footed cachepot or on a raised pedestal on your desk or a tabletop or on a file cabinet. Small plants are great in bookcases, where their fronds can cascade over the edges of shelves.

SITUATIONS WANTED: Temperatures ranging from 70 degrees in the day to 65 degrees at night are ideal for Boston ferns. This particular species will stand temperatures up to perhaps 75 degrees as long as there is lots of moisture in the air and lots of fresh air. Blasts of hot, dry, stale air will ruin both new growth and older fronds very quickly. Light can range from semisunny to semishady, near an east or west window, in a north window, or several feet from a curtained south window. In winter it can acclimatize to southern sun if moved there gradually. It will also do well under fluorescents.

SALARY REQUIREMENTS: Keep the soil evenly moist. If the soil dries out, it will kill fronds in just hours. Mist a Boston fern often—daily if the temperatures are above 70 degrees. Feed all-purpose plant food half as often as container directs. Do not overfeed. The Boston fern doesn't respond well to handling or potting. If it begins to crowd its pot, wait till spring, then lift out root divisions and start these in African violet or terrarium soil. Long hairy strands grow periodically from this kind of fern: If the tips touch soil they will root and start baby plants. If you don't want young plants, cut the runners.

FYI: Blasts of heat and dry stale air ruin ferns.

Pellaea rotundifolia

RESUMÉ: A fascinating rock fern, this plant has delicate blue-green foliage growing on wiry fronds about 12 inches long. It's a little like a maidenhair fern but easier to grow indoors. The overall height is between 4 and 8 inches. The foliage is round when the plants are young and becomes oblong as they mature. The fronds in young plants grow in asymmetrical fashion—some long, some short—then develop into a swirled starfish formation. There are pellaeas that grow wild in America (it's one of the protected species), but *Pellaea rotundifolia* comes from New Zealand, where it grows in limestone caves.

RELOCATION: *P. rotundifolia* is at its best set in a round, shiny, footed container or set on a low pedestal. A charming plant for a corner of a desk, nestled among books in a corner of a book-case, or combined with other small plants whose foliage is upright and a little stiff like holly fern. It looks wonderful in a garden of baby ferns, either in a bookcase shelf growing under fluorescents or in a small planter.

SITUATIONS WANTED: Reference books disagree on how to handle pellaea: Some say the plant likes it dry and sunny, others recommend it have dim light and moisture. Dagny Hansen, at Plant Specialists in New York, succeeds with pellaea in good light a few feet from an east or west window (not direct sun) or in a bright north window. She says it can handle an hour or two of direct sun each day if you are careful to keep the soil evenly moist and mist often. She also grows pellaea directly under fluorescent lights. Best temperatures are between 55 and 70 degrees, although the plants can stand a slightly higher temperature if the room is aired and the plants misted often.

SALARY REQUIREMENTS: Keep the soil evenly moist; empty the saucer one hour after watering. Mist the plant daily when new. Feed all-purpose plant food half as often as directed. If the container becomes crowded, repot in half-and-half all-purpose soil and ground humus. Add limestone—as directed on the package—to sweeten the soil.

FYI: Hot, dry, stale air and too much direct sun can ruin the plant.

Peperomia Species

RESUMÉ: These are small, low-growing, slow-growing tropicals of many different kinds, great for overheated offices. The types most familiar, like *Peperomia sandersii* (the watermelon begonia) have rounded or heart-shaped silver-striped foliage and crimson stems. Another large group has stiff waxy succulentlike leaves. Typical of this kind are *P. obtusifolia* and its white-edged variation, *P. o. variegata*. There are some dainty, small-leaved creepers like *P. rotundifolia* and *P. prostrata*. All are compact indoor plants.

RELOCATION: When you are growing only one, show it off in a small pot; two, three, or more types make a neat dish garden. Or, grow a couple of peperomias, for instance, *P. sandersii* and *P. obtusifolia*, in a big dish garden with plants such as small *Dieffenbachia* (page 74), small-leaved English ivies (*Hedera helix*, page 131), *Dracaena sanderiana* (page 43), and *Aglaonema* (page 26). Single plants or pairs of peperomias are great under a lamp on a desk; dish gardens with peperomias are especially beautiful when lighted from above so that their silver stripes and other variegations can shine.

SITUATIONS WANTED: The peperomias can stand high temperatures—between 65 and 85 degrees. They manage in a broad range of light conditions, too, from filtered southern sunlight to a 75-watt desk lamp as far as 3 feet away. Fluorescents supply enough light, near or far, and light a few feet from an east, west, or north window or right in a north window is ample.

SALARY REQUIREMENTS: If the soil gets too dry, the leaves will fall fast. If it is kept too moist, the roots will rot. Water only when the surface soil begins to feel dry, then water thoroughly and empty the saucer an hour later. Mist occasionally if the temperatures are on the high side. Feed all-purpose plant food half as often as directed or less if light is low. Repot only if container is crowded, in all-purpose soil with 2 inches of pebbles in the bottom for drainage. You can root 3-inch tip cuttings in all-purpose soil to start new plants.

FYI: Soil kept soggy or dry is bad news.

Pilea cadierei
ALUMINUM PLANT

RESUMÉ: There are several kinds of pilea, all tropical plants with silvery markings similar to peperomia (page 51) of the watermelon begonia type. Like peperomias, pileas like it hot. Most suppliers offer the standard-size aluminum plant, a fast grower that gets to be about 18 inches tall with quilted leaves marked evenly with silver. There's a darling dwarf, *Pilea cadierei* 'Minima,' whose leaves are olive green with raised areas marked silver and pink stems. You'll find that suppliers usually carry at least two other pileas: *P. involucrata*, friendship plant; and *P. microphylla*, artillery plant or artillery fern. *P. microphylla* is attractive, but it's an annual; *P. cadierei* is a perennial.

RELOCATION: The dwarf 'Minima' is a showy plant for a small space. The standard size is especially handsome in a tall narrow container, and it is a good backgrounder for a planter edged with low cascading foliage like wandering jew (*Tradescantia*, page 138). Light pilea so that the foliage shows its silver. Low growers are great in terrariums and bottle gardens.

SITUATIONS WANTED: Pileas can take 80- to 85-degree temperatures during the day, and they like it best when night levels are 62 to 65 degrees, but they'll manage very well in a steady 70 degrees. Good exposures are a few feet back from a bright east or west window, in a north window, in a venetian-blinded south window, or under overhead fluorescents. Try 'Minima' under a 75-watt desk light. If the leaves pale, lessen the light.

SALARY REQUIREMENTS: Mist often. Water when the soil feels dry on the surface, and don't let the soil dry out. An hour after watering, empty the saucer. Grow pilea on a saucer filled with moist pebbles. Feed all-purpose plant food half as often as package directs. When the plant outgrows its container, repot in three parts all-purpose soil and one part humus, or in terrarium soil. You can root 3-inch tip cuttings to make new plants.

FYI: If the soil dries or if you keep it soggy, you will probably lose the plant. Cold drafts may wither it.

Plectranthus australis
SWEDISH IVY

RESUMÉ: Round, shiny, bright green leaves that grow thickly on four-sided jointed cascading stems—that's Swedish ivy. In low light it grows slowly, making it a perfect candidate for desk space. In bright light, it grows rather quickly into a big, beautiful basket plant. Dealers offer plain green sorts, but there are white-splashed types of *Plectranthus australis* and its bronzy relative, *P. oertendahlii*. Some sources claim that *P. oertendahlii* is the only species correctly called Swedish ivy (actually the plant is a mint from India and came to us by way of great popularity in Sweden), but the name has stuck to all the Plectranthus species.

RELOCATION: Baby plants look great in small round pots raised just enough so that the young stems can cascade. They brighten bookcase nooks and washroom ledges. The first one I ever met lived, almost unchanged, for years in a pocket in a handsome antique wood end table in a dim reception room. Big plants are great hanging or on a pedestal.

SITUATIONS WANTED: In Sweden the indoors in winter is between 65 and 68 degrees; there Swedish ivy thrives. However, it's okay at 70 degrees and a little higher if there's lots of fresh air. Bright light near east, west, or in a north window is fine, or near a shuttered south window. Under a 75-watt desk lamp, young plants maintain their size but don't grow much. Large plants, once acclimated, succeed under fluorescents.

SALARY REQUIREMENTS: Keep the soil evenly moist, not soggy. Water when the surface begins to feel dry. In low light, water plants less, but never let them go bone dry. Feed all-purpose plant food half as often as package directs. Repot annually in all-purpose soil with gravel in the pot bottom for drainage. Summered in low light, they will cover themselves with tiny white flowers that end up making a big mess! Keep growing plants pinched back to encourage compactness or the plants lose their beauty. Root tip cuttings in vermiculite or water. Swedish ivy goes past its prime in two or three years, so start replacement plants annually.

FYI: Bone dry soil and high heat can kill.

Polypodium aureum mandaianum
HARE'S-FOOT FERN

RESUMÉ: The edges of this bluish fern are crisp and irregularly toothed, hard to describe, and striking to see. This is perhaps the easiest to grow and most popular of the big ferns used commercially. The common name, hare's-foot fern, refers to the rhizome (root + stem), which is hairy, cinnamon-colored, and good-looking. Some sources call this particular species bear's-paw fern because of its size. When young, with the first fronds just beginning in a pot, it is a striking desk plant. Mature, it makes a glorious pedestal plant or basket plant, to feature alone or group with other plants.

RELOCATION: Feature young plants under a tall spotlight, on your desk, in a north window, or as a busy asymmetrical backdrop for small round plants (like Swedish ivy, page 53). Large plants are great on pedestals anywhere high up where the foliage can be seen and can cascade freely downward. You may mass several together in a big planter or group three or four together atop a big file cabinet as an office divider.

SITUATIONS WANTED: Like other ferns, this species needs a cool climate. The ideal is 70 degrees during the day and a little cooler at night, but below 55 degrees there will be trouble. No direct sun is the rule, but a spot near a sunny east or west window is very good and so are overhead fluorescents. Young plants should adapt under a tall (2- to 2½-feet) desk lamp with 75-watt bulbs or under overhead 150-watt floods if they receive some light from nearby windows as well.

SALARY REQUIREMENTS: Keep the soil evenly moist but never soggy. Empty the saucer one hour after watering. If the light is quite low, water less often. If temperatures are warmer than 70 degrees, mist often. A monthly shower will do a great deal to freshen the plant since the broad fronds collect dust. Feed all-purpose plant food half as often as package directs. Repot in all-purpose plant food when the fern outgrows its pot; place 2 inches of small gravel in the bottom of the pot to insure good drainage.

FYI: Blasts of hot, dry air can ruin a beautiful fern, young or old, though this type can stand it better than most.

Pteris Species
TABLE FERN

RESUMÉ: These attractive airy plants were the standbys of our great-grandmothers' table ferns, or brakes, grown in cool dim parlors. Though the fronds differ from species to species, the growth habit of most kinds is similar: asymmetrical, irregular, and all mixed up in the color and size and length. These characteristics make for a dynamic look quite unlike the tidy Boston fern and exciting. Some species have weird unfernlike fronds: *Pteris cretica*, for instance, has fronds like ribbons on straw-colored stems. Suppliers are more likely to carry *P. ensiformis*, the sword brake, or the graceful narrow *P. multifida*, which is one of the best ferns for dish gardens. The frond lengths of most species stay to about 20 inches, and the plants offered usually are a foot or so tall.

RELOCATION: A single young pteris makes a whole desk garden once it gets going, but young plants are also good-looking in big dish gardens and terrariums. Group it with species of contrasting foliage, or combine it with prayer plant. A north window with no direct sun makes a good home for such a group; so does a big file cabinet under overhead fluorescents.

SITUATIONS WANTED: A cool place of 68 to 70 degrees (not below 55) with no direct sun is an ideal situation for the table fern. Most other ferns can be moved into a little direct sun and eventually will tolerate quite a lot of direct sun—but not the table fern. Otherwise it's adaptable. Though it responds to the moisture of a terrarium, it also stands up very well to dry office climates.

SALARY REQUIREMENTS: Keep the soil evenly moist. Make sure you empty the pot saucer of excess water an hour after watering. Mist often when temperatures go above 70 degrees, and feed all-purpose plant food half as often as directed. When container becomes crowded, repot in three parts all-purpose soil and one part humus, or in terrarium soil. Shower the plant occasionally if you can, and it will be prettier and healthier.

FYI: Blasts of hot dry air or direct sun can be harmful.

Sansevieria trifasciata 'Hahnii'
SNAKE PLANT

RESUMÉ: Sansevieria is another of those so-often-seen, so-indestructible plants that aren't used to their full capacity. The best-known sansevieria is *Sansevieria thyrsiflora*, whose pointed dark green leaves, banded like snakeskin, spear straight up from the soil in a cluster. *S. trifasciata* 'Hahnii' produces a low rosette of this type of foliage: The leaf tips spiral like a pinwheel and are beautifully banded in light green. 'Golden Hahnii' has broad edgings and bands of gold on dark green; 'Silver Hahnii' is decked in metallic white that looks silvery in strong light.

RELOCATION: 'Hahnii' is a decorative and imperturbable desk ornament likely to multiply itself fairly quickly. It is great alone in a glossy low ceramic container or as the focal point of a dish garden. It combines well with pastel sedums (*Dracaena sanderiana*, page 43) and the small-leaved ivy, *Hedera helix* 'Hahn's Star,' page 131—all have similar watering and soil needs. Light for a dish garden containing these plants could be fluorescents or a few feet back from a sunny east or west window. 'Golden Hahnii' backed by any of the tall sansevierias makes a great planter garden for the reluctant gardener.

SITUATIONS WANTED: Sansevieria will adapt to almost any situation. Temperatures up to 80 degrees and even above during the day and down to 65 or 62 degrees at night are okay. Light can be filtered or sunny; sansevieria adapts to fluorescents, a desk lamp, or north or south windows.

SALARY REQUIREMENTS: Sansevierias look most beautiful if the soil is kept moderately damp. When watering, drench the soil until water fills the saucer. An hour later, empty the saucer. Don't water too often; the soil should get slightly dry between waterings. Feed all-purpose plant food half as often as package directs. When the container becomes crowded, repot in all-purpose soil with 1 or 2 inches of small gravel in the pot bottom to insure good drainage. Remove and plant suckers when you repot or when you want new baby plants. Wipe the foliage with a wet cloth monthly to keep it looking its best.

FYI: Waterlogged soil can kill sansevieria.

Saxifraga sarmentosa
STRAWBERRY BEGONIA
STRAWBERRY GERANIUM

RESUMÉ: This is one of the most adorable creepers around. The word *strawberry* refers to its habit of putting out long wiry runners that bear tiny plantlets. The leaves are hairy, round, and reminiscent of begonia or geranium leaves—deep green with silvered areas backed by maroon. At maturity the plants are only 4 inches high, and they produce clusters of white flowers. There's a smaller, showier, more difficult variety (better in a terrarium) called 'Tricolor.' *Saxifraga sarmentosa* is also known as S. stolonifera.

RELOCATION: A young plant in a white pot is delightful under a desk lamp with 60-watt bulbs. Several, each on its own little pedestal or all together in a big dish garden or terrarium, make a lovely display. When the runners grow long, the plants will need to be raised higher: Move to a book shelf or file cabinet.

SITUATIONS WANTED: Fragile as it looks, this is a successful office worker as long as it can stay cool. Cool here means 65 to 68 degrees; okay, too, at 70 degrees as long as the room is aired and airy (get air from the air conditioner if you have no windows) and the plant is often misted. The light source can be a few feet from an east or west window, in a north window, fluorescents, or incandescent bulbs in a desk lamp. The less light, the more slowly the plant will grow.

SALARY REQUIREMENTS: Let the plant become moderately dry between waterings, then drench until excess seeps into the saucer. Wait for an hour, then empty the saucer. If the plant is growing in a dish garden or a terrarium, be careful not to let the soil be constantly soaked. 'Tricolor,' in particular, won't stand for soggy soil. Feed all-purpose plant food half as often as package directs. Mist daily and air the room often, especially if temperatures are over 70 degrees. When containers become crowded, repot in all-purpose potting soil with pebbles for drainage. You can root plantlets growing on the runners by pressing the plantlets gently into a pot of soil *without removing them from the parent plant.* When the plantlets are well enough rooted to resist a slight tug, cut them free of the runners.

FYI: Soggy soil and hot drafts can ruin saxifraga.

Tolmiea menziesii
PIGGYBACK PLANT

RESUMÉ: The piggyback plant is a lush bouquet of fresh green leaves. It's called piggyback because tiny baby plants grow, piggyback fashion, on the surface of older leaves where they join their stems. Young plants become full plants rather quickly and top out at about 12 inches high.

RELOCATION: Big for a table plant, a young tolmiea is all a desk needs to have that green-grows-my-garden look. A single mature plant under a tall spot or desk lamp on an end table will do a great deal for a small reception area. A few mature plants can cover the top of a file cabinet.

SITUATIONS WANTED: Tolmiea does best at 70 degrees with cooler nights (to 55 degrees). Fresh humid air makes it flourish. It grows beautifully under fluorescents and manages well when young under spot lights or lamps with 75-watt incandescent bulbs, as long as the lamps aren't close enough to overheat the area. Near a bright east or west window or in a north window are good locations for tolmiea.

SALARY REQUIREMENTS: Keep the soil evenly moist. Don't let it dry out or leaf edges will brown. If you are a neglectful gardener, grow several tolmieas on a tray of moist pebbles to insure humidity. Water till excess flows into the saucer; wait an hour, then empty the saucer. Mist often (daily if temperatures are over 70 degrees), and provide fresh air if you can. Repot as soon as the container shows signs of crowding. Cramped plants don't last as long as plants that are repotted often. Use all-purpose soil and layer the pot bottom with pebbles to guarantee good drainage. Tolmieas play out after a year or so, but you can start new plants by rooting 3-inch tip cuttings of leaves bearing babies. Use vermiculite for the rooting process, then transfer the plants to all-purpose soil.

FYI: Crowded pots, dry soil, hot drafts are no-nos for the moisture-loving tolmieas.

3
The Shrubs

The shrubs in an office usually are "management" plants. That is, they're big enough to occupy key positions, so management has to want them before you can install them. And they are costly enough to make you think twice about spending your own money to buy them. Since they are real investments, it pays to know how to buy and handle them.

Some plants used as shrubs are real shrubs—by dictionary definition a multi-stemmed plant that stays under 15 feet grown outdoors. Other plants sold as shrubs are rather small trees than shrubs; they may be young, they may have been dwarfed by small containers, or they may be small because they are growing in low light, less than their native condition. It pays to know which is which so that you will have a notion about its eventual size.

Buying

Some shrub-size plants are less costly than others. You can buy small plants of fast-growing shrubs and trees for relatively little money. When you are dealing with plants, one general rule is that the more mature (bigger) the plant, the more you pay. (The cost of a tree is often estimated by linear foot.) Another general rule is that the more slowly the plant grows, the more it costs. This is logical since the grower has put more time and

1 *Rhapis excelsa*; 2 *Ficus lyrata*; 3 *Scindapsus aureus*; 4 *Hedera helix*;
5 *Philodendron selloum*; 6 *Pittosporum tobira*

money into getting a slow grower to mature size than a fast grower. Ask the price before you order the goods. You can't tell just by looking what the cost will be.

Containers

The cost of large plants doesn't end with the purchase price of the plants themselves, for these are usually sold potted in green metal or plastic tubs that contribute nothing to the office decor. To set a shrub off beautifully, you need an attractive container for the tub, perhaps a cachepot. Or if you prefer to spend your shrub allowance on the plant itself, you can make a plain-jane tub into a work of art by painting it—water-base paint will do— and then overpainting with a bright Indian blanket pattern; covering the tub with an attractive water resistant paper; or if you're really handy, you can get into rope tricks by winding thick twine round and round the tub. But even if you are going to make do with the original tub, you still must buy a saucer to go under it, for without it, you'll flood the floor each time you water the plant.

The best saucers are soft, rubberlike plastic. They are commonly sold in greens and terracotta colors. You may paint the outside to match the tub and fill the inside with pretty river-washed, buff-colored or white pebbles—an addition that helps keep moisture around the plant.

One of the least expensive types of cachepots is a woven basket. Prices range from $10 to tens of dollars. Before you buy, make sure the basket will be big enough to contain the saucer. If you put the basket in the saucer, in time it will rot. A basket tall enough to come up to 2 to 4 inches above the tub top sets the foliage off beautifully.

Still reasonable in price and practical are plain white plastic cylinders sold as cachepots. These double as saucers and give a crisp finish to the plant. They are particularly attractive against dark floors, and I've never yet had one that leaked. There are also inexpensive black plastic cachepots, but these don't seem to show off the plants as nicely.

Mexican pottery imports and plain-jane terracotta cachepots are handsome too but as a rule cost more than plastic. Pottery with unglazed bottoms and the terracotta type absorb and hold moisture. You can waterproof the bottoms by painting them with several coats of polyurethane. But I'd hesitate to place pottery waterproofed in this fashion on an expensive tabletop or rug. A pet ficus in a pet pottery urn once ruined a pet oriental belonging to my mother. Remember, too, that even painted metal surfaces can rust.

If you are planning to transplant your shrub to another pot rather than place the original tub inside a cachepot, be aware that this is costly, too. You can pay as much as $30 for a simple 18-inch terracotta pot. A white plastic pot the same size costs about one-fifth as much.

To give you a notion of pot sizes needed for large plants, as a rule you need an 8-inch pot for a young southern yew (*Podocarpus macrophylla maki*) and a 15-inch pot for a dwarf date palm such as *Phoenix roebelenii*. The way pots are measured, by the way, is across the top—the diameter, not the circumference: The height equals the diameter for standard-shaped pots but is less in the type called bulb pan or azalea pot.

If economy is not your business, there are some elegant plant containers in which to invest: Magnificently patterned china water jugs, sculptured Japanese urns, polished aluminum cubes, gloriously colorful monotone ceramics are just a few.

Pedestals

A young shrub doubles as a tree if you place it on a table or file cabinet. The alternative is to buy a pedestal. Well-woven, upended baskets are sturdy enough to act as pedestals. There are also reasonably priced rope plant stands and attractive clear or colored plastic cubes. Next in line of cost are wooden, then aluminum pedestals, and after that the sky's the limit as far as the price goes.

Decorating

Shrubs are middle-size plants, versatile, and indispensible in an office garden. A couple of shrubs of different heights set on the floor bring grace to a tree that when placed alone tends to be forlorn and leggy. A single shrub is a perfect backdrop for a floor garden of small plants.

Shrubs with either identical, similar, or contrasting foliage set on pedestals of different heights make attractive displays. Spot several shrubs on top of tall file cabinets in a big work room, the effect being the creation of a woodland for much less than it would cost to bring in trees. Up high, shrubs get light from all the windows.

Shrubs set on a pebble bed in a big wooden planter make a delightful area divider, a reception room display, or a great corridor cheerer. A planter suitable for shrubs even in small sizes will have to be custom-made to fit the site. The bottom should be lined with a tin tray deep enough to hold 2 inches of pebbles. Most metalworking shops will make a tin tray at moderate cost. And if there isn't such a shop nearby, try a car body repair shop. The tray must be waterproof. Check it out before

1 *Podocarpus macrophylla;* 2 *Ficus elastica decora;* 3 *Philodendron selloum*

you install it. Set the pot bottom directly on the pebbles; in a planter that has pebbles you don't need a saucer.

Another way to use shrubs as a divider is to set a row of big shrubs on pedestals of varying heights. Run them high–medium–low; or one high, one low, peg-leg fashion. I prefer plants with same or similar foliage for this kind of treatment. In the next chapter there are some detailed suggestions for office gardens combining shrubs, trees, and other plants. Furthermore, Chapter 7 offers additional plans for office dividers.

Here are some other ways several shrubs can be used in a group: Combine one tall, one medium, one low; combine one drooping tall plant and two low plants; combine several plants of one kind with contrasting foliage; combine one big-leaved stiff plant, like a young India rubber plant, *Ficus elastica decora*, one big-leaved, low-growing plant, like *Philodendron selloum*, and one feathery plant, like *Podocarpus macrophylla* or *Dizygotheca elegantissima*, or an overgrown fern from among those described in Chapter 2.

When you group shrubs with contrasting foliage to make a garden, use pedestals and containers that harmonize in color and kind. When you mix same or similar foliage shrubs, mix and match contrasting pedestals and containers: Rope and woven baskets harmonize, as do plastic and aluminum, terracotta and pottery, china cachepots and Japanese metal urns.

The Office Climate

Before you put a shrub to work, make sure it is going to do well on the job. Light and temperature are key factors in the success of big plants. The shrubs on the following pages all are successful in temperatures of about 70 degrees, all can take lower night temperatures, a few prefer 65 or 68 to 70 degrees, and several do very well at 80, even 85 degrees.

When looking for a cool spot for a shrub you are interested in, test the area next to the windows. Often it's cooler there. Don't place plants noted for their need for moisture near heat convectors—the air is drier there. Don't place plants that hate cold drafts near air conditioners or windows or doors that open to the outdoors.

Fatsia japonica

Most shrubs can stand a little more heat and a little more cool than indicated, but all benefit from—and some *must* have—misting to increase moisture during the winter heating season.

The alternative to hand misting is an electric humidifier, a good investment in the north, where buildings usually are overheated in winter. There are models available for under $25 which are noisy and need filling once or twice a day. More expensive models require less maintenance.

Another way to increase atmospheric humidity is to group plants on 2 inches of wet pebbles in large trays. The water level must never be even with pot bottoms but well below them. See the discussion on watering large plants, pages 68–69. Observation will tell you how much water each tray needs during the week—more in winter, very little in summer. If the water isn't evaporating within the week, add less. Sitting water becomes stagnant and smells nasty.

Important to many big plants and good for all is fresh air, and it's nice for humans, too. This means opening windows for a few minutes once or twice during the day. Many offices have windows that can't be opened, but that is not necessarily that. There may be an air conditioner that will allow you to draw fresh air from the outside into the room. If there's no way to bring air in, avoid plants that must have fresh air. If you must have that kind of plant, place it where there is traffic, not in a corner or behind a post where air is dead.

Lighting

When you are placing a tall plant, remember that the light it gets in any given spot rarely is limited to the obvious source. Overhead fluorescents are augmented by light from all the windows in the room, and vice versa. In big open offices with windows, some light is reaching every corner of the room most of the day. If you are doubtful that existing light will be enough, add a spotlight or a floodlight. Or, inspire management to install a recessed ceiling spotlight just for a plant. If burning it during the day presents problems, you can turn it on at night before you leave.

Although experts, me included, sound dogmatic about the amount of light a given plant needs, light dogma, like all dogma, is fallible. A plant that grows well in day-long sun from a south window (about 5,600 footcandles of light in winter in New York) may only need 500 to 2,000 footcandles over a 16-hour period to maintain itself very well. Light from a bright east or west window delivers that; add in the overhead fluorescents, and the footcandles of light delivered goes up considerably. I wish I could say exactly how many footcandles of light each plant needs and exactly what combinations of lighting deliver that many footcandles, but footcandles has to do with light intensity, and it varies all over the country and from season to season. Also, each plant's needs are variable, depending on its past history. All anyone can do is give you a notion of the kind of light each plant needs; from there on in you must play it by eye. If new foliage comes in small, pale, widely spaced on weak stems, there's not enough light. Burned, puckered patches on foliage or dried-out new growth usually mean there's too much light. Leaves also tend to pale in excess light.

And here's another thing to consider: Shrubs, given time, acclimate to both less light than they prefer and more light than they usually need. Light shortage, within limits, can be an asset: It slows growth. If you want fast-growing shrubs to remain their present size, give them less light. On the other hand, if you want young shrubs to soar into tree sizes, supply as much light as they can take. Start them in the light suggested, and over a period of weeks, move them closer to the light.

Watering

Where the average desk plant will need weekly ½ to 2 cupfuls of water (make it tepid water, please!), large plants will need 2 cups to a quart (4 cups) or more. They'll require more during active growth, spring usually, and winter if your heat really soars. Plants with lots of thin leaves generally need more water than plants with a few big succulent or evergreen leaves. Big plants need more water than small plants of the same species. Plants in barely enough light need less than the same plants in adequate light because they aren't growing. These are only some generalizations about watering. Only your hand on the soil can tell you whether you are keeping the soil at just the degree of moisture each plant needs. We notice that some shops are beginning to carry moisture-measuring devices, but read Chapter 8 before you run out to buy one.

How do you water the big plants? A 4-, 6-, or 8-quart watering can is as much as I can lift. Someday, perhaps by the time you read this, there will be an indoor hose on the market. (Those sold now are tiny, so don't buy one until the dealer shows you that it delivers water fast enough to make it worth having!)

Pour water onto the soil until it begins to seep into the saucer, and allow the plant to sit in the excess water for one hour. By then it has reabsorbed as much water as it needs. After that, you must drain the saucer; if it holds pebbles, bring the level of the water in the saucer below the pot bottom. That's easy with a small plant, but big plants are too heavy to lift. You can draw excess water off with a bulb baster, or you can scoop it up with a small cup. But there's even an easier alternative: When a new plant arrives, measure how much water you pour on and how much the plant reabsorbs in an hour. Thereafter you can water the plant accordingly.

Plants that are allowed to dry out somewhat between waterings usually drink up more saucer water than those kept evenly moist. When you first install one of these, keep refilling the saucer as it empties for an hour and note how much the plant actually absorbs. Colored labels on each of the big pots indicating exactly how much water the plants use make life easier.

Feeding

The effect of overfeeding plants is salt buildup in the soil. This is offset for small plants by repotting. Repotting a shrub is a chore, though, and repotting a tree is a major and messy undertaking. So—don't overfeed big plants. Feed at half the rate recommended on package labels even in periods of active growth. When you add food to the watering can, make the measure scant! Plants in barely enough light to maintain themselves and plants not growing either because it's winter or because they are sulking should be fed hardly at all; three or four times a year will be plenty.

Large shrubs and trees in pots 15 to 19 inches, for instance, benefit from an annual top dressing of fresh soil. The process is explained in the next chapter.

Selection

The plants on the following pages are generally offered in sizes ranging from about 30 inches tall to 3 or 4 feet or more. Although big sizes make instant gardens, small sizes not only cost less but are better able to acclimate to office conditions. All the plants here are durable; they're the very toughest of their kind as well as the most attractive.

In California some of the plants described in the next chapter as trees are sold in shrub sizes; among them are small scheffleras of several kinds, and the kentia palm (*Howeia fosteriana*). In

California you will also find shrub sizes of *Tupidanthus calyptratus*, a small evergreen that responds to warmth and moisture.

If you are in the south and your office offers a partially shaded patio or terrace on which plants can vacation, you may also add to my list some of the lovely citruses: calamondin (*Citrus mitis*) ; the American wonder-lemon (*Citrus limonia* 'Ponderosa'), which actually produces lemons; the colorful crotons (*Codiaeum*) ; and *Gardenia jasminoides*. These can make it indoors if they can summer out.

Two good indoor shrubs that I have not included because they are hard to find are the natal plum (*Carissa grandiflora*) and miniature holly (*Malpighia coccigera*).

The Plants

Chamaedorea elegans 'Bella'
NEANTHE BELLA PALM

RESUMÉ: This is a miniature tree palm, a single slender reed-like green stem topped by a graceful fan of fronds. A dwarf of the 8-foot-tall parlor palm, *Chamaedorea elegans*, neanthe bella usually stays at 3 or 4 feet. In California it is sold in sizes that fit 6-inch pots and is used as a table and sill plant. And in California young plants of two other species, *C. costaricana* and *C. seifrizii*, are sold as shrubs. All the chamaedoreas are very easy to grow and are good choices where warm air and dim light are the rule.

RELOCATION: Nice in baskets or rope cachepots, this palm adds a touch of the exotic and has a rather formal look. Young neanthe bellas are small enough for use in groups in big planters. A large specimen is quite imposing alone in a reception room. Or, use it as the focus of a garden in a lobby.

SITUATIONS WANTED: Neanthe bellas come from Guatemala and can stand a lot of warmth: 80 to 85 degrees won't phase them as long as the soil is moist. And they can withstand temperatures as low as 65 degrees. They are adaptable to various lights but avoid placing them in direct sunlight: Try to the side or a few feet back from an east, west, or in a north window; under overhead fluorescents; or under a 150-watt incandescent spot. Baby plants should adapt to fairly low light on your desk and do very well in a terrarium under fluorescents.

SALARY REQUIREMENTS: Keep the soil evenly moist; water often (about 2 to 3 cups twice a week for a 3- to 4-foot plant), but don't drench the plant. Mist daily or as often as possible. If the soil dries out, leaf tips and whole fronds will yellow; you can groom away the spoiled areas with scissors. If a frond goes, use scissors to cut the leaf stem from the main stem. New fronds sometimes need help to open up: Gently pull individual tips one from the other. Feed half as much all-purpose plant food as package directs. Every year top dress with three parts all-purpose soil and one part peat moss. Sponge the fronds occasionally.

FYI: Red spider mites attack in hot dry air.

Chamaerops humilis
EUROPEAN FAN PALM

RESUMÉ: This imposing durable palm from the Mediterranean area is a better choice than neanthe bella palm if yours is a cool office. The plant is bushy, sometimes growing in a clump, sometimes as a single stalk about 3 feet tall. The fronds open into broad, rounded fans of leaves. Older specimens often have single thick trunks topped by graceful clusters of leaves with low stems coming up from the bases, each with several fronds. They are quite beautiful.

RELOCATION: Young plants are attractive in ornate iron or glazed ceramic cachepots; older plants demand glamorous containers—a low, colorful Chinese water jar, for instance. Five or six fan palms of different sizes make a striking display for a roomy reception area. Half a dozen young plants in a big, low, oblong planter make a fine room divider. A single mature plant is a good backdrop for a group of big, low-growing shrubs with tropical foliage, like *Philodendron selloum* (page 82).

SITUATIONS WANTED: This palm is happiest in 70-degree days and can go to 55 degrees and lower at night. The fan palm needs fresh air and suffers near heat convectors. Ideal light includes some direct sun, an hour or two each day, from an east or west window. It adapts to a half-sunny south window and thrives in a north window, especially if there is additional light from an overhead fluorescent. Fluorescent spots, grow-light spots, or a pair of high-up incandescent spots with 150-watt bulbs should each be enough if placed so that light falls directly on the plant.

SALARY REQUIREMENTS: The fan palm likes soil quite moist, even wet, so water thoroughly and often. If the plant is in a low light, water less. Stand the pot on a bed of moist pebbles and mist often to improve humidity. Feed half as much all-purpose plant food as package directs. Every year top dress with three parts all-purpose soil and one part peat moss.

FYI: Red spider mites are a hazard in hot dry air; frequent misting should keep them away.

Cycas revoluta
SAGO PALM

RESUMÉ: Tall, stiff, drooping fronds with leaves all the way down the stem, like a fern, make this something of a contrast to the round-fronded fan palm. Actually, sago palm doesn't belong to the palm family; it's just a pretend palm, older than history. Outdoors in Japan, it grows to 10 feet, topped by fronds 5 feet long; there the male tree produces a 2-foot red cone right at the top of the thick trunk. The plants are slow growers. Young plants sold for indoor culture have only the fernlike fronds and are good, enduring office plants.

RELOCATION: A young plant looks best in a tall, rather massive cachepot. Use several young sago palms in a big, low planter or grouped, each on a pedestal of different height. Maturing sago palm is wonderful in a floor garden with big jade plants, fan palms, and thick-leaved shrubs, such as false aralia (page 75) or a grown-up *Fatsia japonica* (page 78).

SITUATIONS WANTED: Happiest in 70-degree temperatures the palm can survive nights as low as 55 degrees. It can take slightly higher heats (above 70 degrees) if misted and aired often. Best light is a few hours of sun in an east or west window or a venetian-blinded south window, if not too hot. A bright north window, fluorescent overheads, or 150-watt floods are satisfactory, too. This plant is reasonably adaptable.

SALARY REQUIREMENTS: Allow the soil to become moderately dry before watering, then drench. Don't leave excess water in the saucer for more than an hour. Calculate how much water poured through the plant will fill the saucer, how much the plant reabsorbs in an hour, and add that much each time. Water less in winter but mist and air daily. Feed all-purpose plant food half as often as package directs, and top dress the soil every year with three parts all-purpose soil and one part peat. Wipe the fronds with a wet sponge every few months. Be careful of the tips: They're sharp!

FYI: Hot dry air and soggy soil spoil the plant. If the atmosphere is consistently hot and dry, red spider mites will probably attack.

Dieffenbachia Species
DUMBCANE

RESUMÉ: These are small shrubs, moderately fast growing, with big, thin leaves spectacularly marked with white, yellow, or chartreuse. (Some species of Aglaonema and Scindapsus are look-alikes.) The leaves of dumbcane are pointed, long, and grow from a central stem. Among the most thrilling varieties are *Dieffenbachia* 'Exotica' and 'Mary Weidner'; both are good choices for small spaces since they stay compact. 'Rudolf Roehrs,' a variety of *D. picta*, is particularly suitable if you're short of light. It has chartreuse markings on green, a lovely combination.

RELOCATION: These showy low shrubs are great anywhere alone, but I think they are super when several of either similar or constrasting markings are grouped in a floor garden or set on pedestals of different heights. A planterful of young dumbcanes looks great in the reception area, in the washroom (the white tiles set off their colors), or used as a divider in an office of moderate size. As the plants grow they get leggy, so stake them and let them grow to small tree size if you like their looks. Or air-layer to start new small plants.

SITUATIONS WANTED: Dumbcane is a tropical plant and can take up to 85 degrees during the day and as low as 65 degrees at night. A spot where there is little sun a few feet from an east or west window is okay; so is a bright north window. Overhead fluorescents, spots, or floods with 150-watt bulbs are fine, particularly for varieties of *D. picta*.

SALARY REQUIREMENTS: Don't water dumbcane until the surface soil begins to feel dry. Then drench the plant until water fills the saucer. An hour later, empty the saucer. Don't let the plant sit in a puddle; it doesn't like soggy soil. Mist daily, or often, in winter. Feed all-purpose plant food half as often as directed on the package; top dress yearly with all-purpose soil. Wipe the leaves monthly with a damp cloth; stake the plant if it begins to tilt.

FYI: The stem juice is poisonous. Red spider mites attack in hot, dry, airless rooms.

Dizygotheca elegantissima
FALSE ARALIA

RESUMÉ: This is an airy, lacy-leaved plant 3 to 4 feet tall and one of the prettiest shrubs for the office. The shape is treelike; there are several straight-up stems, like delicate trunks, and from them droop big, deeply cut, red-tinted leaves that are truly elegant. Marvelously adaptable to any light, *Dizygotheca elegantissima* is one of the most durable of the shrub-size plants. If you are ordering this plant, be sure to specify it by its horticultural name; *Fatsia japonica,* which has much coarser leaves, is also called aralia. If you are on a budget, try to find a young plant and let it grow up to fill your need. False aralia requires time to adjust to new situations and usually drops some leaves in the process, but once acclimated, it will grow well.

RELOCATION: A big, white plastic cylinder 15 inches wide is a great cachepot for false aralia; it also looks very well in any type of basket or rope cachepot. A single mature plant will dress up a reception area, do wonders for a washroom, or soften the corner of a dreary hall. A row of aralia makes a light, airy room divider. It looks nice grouped with a mature *Fatsia japonica* (page 78) and a big jade plant (*Crassula argentea,* pages 38–39) ; elevated on a pedestal, false aralia doubles as a tree.

SITUATIONS WANTED: False aralia can endure high temperatures during the day but will do best if nights are cool, even as low as 65 degrees. Ideal light includes one or two hours of sun a few feet from an east or west window, and it will adapt to anything except a hot south window. Fluorescents or any lights bright enough to read by are fine, especially if the light is reflected by white walls or mirrors. Overhead spotlights, one or two, depending on the breadth of the plant, are probably all you need. Remember to be patient, though; false aralia takes time to adapt.

SALARY REQUIREMENTS: Keep the soil evenly moist but not soggy. Water it often but not too well. Mist daily if you can— it thrives in moist air—and air the room as often as possible. Top dress every 6 or 12 months with all-purpose soil; feed all-purpose plant food half as often as the package recommends.

FYI: Dry soil and hot drafts can spoil the plant.

Dracaena deremensis warneckei

RESUMÉ: The dracaenas are (mostly) tall growers with sword-shaped foliage rather like corn plants'. Some are plain green, like *Dracaena fragrans*, the common corn plant, and some have broad stripes or edgings in gold or white or gray green. *D. deremensis warneckei* is a fresh green, streaked gray green in the center, with two wide white stripes on the edges. A young plant usually is 2 to 2½ feet tall and grows as high as 15 feet in a few years. During that time, it may turn gawky: air-layering will provide another plant as well as solve that problem. In California *D. f. massangeana*, which has a broad yellow center stripe, is sold in shrub sizes. Any dracaena is a great choice for the nervous gardener.

1 *Philodendron oxycardium;* **2** *Dracaena deremensis warneckei*

RELOCATION: Plants 2 to 3 feet tall in big red or blue glazed ceramic containers are decorative in a reception area. *D. fragrans* looks wonderful in a white plastic pot. Dracaena's fountaining foliage goes well with Chinese evergreens (page 26), ferns, and cathedral windows (page 35). If a tall dracaena loses its bottom foliage, grow *Philodendron oxycardium* (page 134) up the stalk.

SITUATIONS WANTED: Hot air and dim light don't phase dracaenas, particularly *D. d. warneckei* and *D. fragrans*. They survive temperatures to 80 or 85 degrees during the day and lows to 65 degrees at night. Filtered light near an east or west window, a few feet from a shuttered south window, or right in a north window are all okay. Dracaeas are fine under overhead fluorescents, too, or beneath overhead incandescent light if you can add an additional 75-watt spotlight, which should burn all day.

SALARY REQUIREMENTS: Keep the soil quite moist, but don't let the dracaena sit in stagnant water. Don't let the soil dry out either; the foliage tops will permanently brown and spoil the plant. Sponge the leaves monthly. Mist occasionally. Feed all-purpose plant food half as often as package instructs. As roots crowd the containers, repot young shrubs in all-purpose soil over 2 inches of drainage pebbles. Top dress big plants annually with all-purpose soil.

FYI: Dry soil ruins leaf tips.

Fatsia japonica and *Fatshedera lizei*

RESUMÉ: This is a bold-leaved plant from Japan, handsome on tables in small 12-inch sizes, great as a shrub when it grows up, a process that will take a couple of years. Each glossy green leaf looks a little like a big, thick maple leaf. *Fatsia japonica* crossed with English ivy produces the popular *Fatshedera lizei* (sometimes called aralia ivy), which can stand a little less light than fatsia. There are very pretty cream and green variegated forms of both plants. Fatshedera tends to vine, while fatsia makes a big, bushy shrub that's more useful at work.

RELOCATION: Fatsia is a stately plant with a lot of presence. Great when you want a bold plant, one that stands out—as on an end table in a reception area or on a worktable in a large space. Variegated fatshedera trained to a trellis is striking. Fatsia and fatshedera are good choices when you needs plants for a cold spot.

SITUATIONS WANTED: Cool and bright but indirect light are the main requirements of both fatsia and fatshedera. Above 70 degrees, fatsia suffers, but it can stand a light frost. Fatshedera is even hardier. Fresh air (from an open window or an air conditioner) is another please-try requirement for fatsia. Light can be supplied by two to three hours of direct sun in winter, but strong indirect light at the side of a sunny window, for instance, is better. Young plants generally adapt to bright overhead fluorescents and to strong light from an incandescent lamp or spotlight.

SALARY REQUIREMENTS: Keep the soil evenly moist and mist the plant occasionally, especially if temperatures are regularly over 68 degrees. Air often if you can. Feed all-purpose plant food half as often as the container directs. Repot in all-purpose potting soil annually or if it outgrows its container. When your table plant begins to outgrow its pot, wait for spring, root 6-inch tip cuttings in vermiculite, then transplant to all-purpose soil, and you'll have new young plants for table or desk use.

FYI: Red spider mites can be a hazard when temperatures are high. Mist and air often.

Ficus elastica
INDIA RUBBER PLANT

RESUMÉ: A tall plant with big rubbery leaves, this is one of the most durable of indoor growers. The large oval leaves climb symmetrically up a sturdy stem until, in time, the plant becomes a single-stemmed tree. There are several varieties, some with colorful foliage. *Ficus elastica decora* is available in California and has bold, broad, deep, glossy green leaves, tipped with red and an ivory midrib that is red beneath. *F. e.* 'Doescheri' is variegated white to cream yellow with a pink midrib and stalk. Outdoors this plant branches and becomes remarkably handsome. It can be beautiful indoors, too, if it is loved.

RELOCATION: This is an imposing plant, even in shrub size. It demands a spot by itself, but in a big area it can be used in neat rows. Take the trouble to place and light a single plant so it casts a shadow; the effect enhances the plant and is quite dramatic. The India rubber plant has a tropical look and is particularly attractive in cane or bamboo cachepots and with an oriental decor.

SITUATIONS WANTED: *F. elastica* is native to India and Malaya and takes high temperatures—to 80—with equanimity. Lows shouldn't be below 65 degrees. Best in some direct sun a few feet back from a big east or west window, several feet from a south window, or right in a bright north window. If leaves of a new plant are yellowing and dropping and new foliage is smaller, add a spotlight.

SALARY REQUIREMENTS: Keep the soil evenly moist but not soggy. Add water till it seeps into the saucer, but remove excess after an hour. Don't let the plant dry out for foliage will yellow and fall. A light mulch of pretty pebbles or woods moss helps. If your office is hot, mist and supply fresh air as often as you can. As it outgrows its container, repot in all-purpose soil over 2 inches of gravel for drainage. Top dress large plants annually, using all-purpose soil. Feed all-purpose plant food half as often as container directs. Monthly, sponge the foliage clean.

FYI: Lack of light and dry or soggy soil cause leaves to drop.

Ficus lyrata
FIDDLELEAF FIG

RESUMÉ: This member of the fig clan has bold, wavy, deeply quilted leathery leaves, shaped a little like fiddles. The color is a dramatic waxy green with yellow veins. Outdoors, in its native West Africa, the plant grows to 40 feet. Indoors, in time, the shrub becomes a small, densely topped little tree. *Ficus lyrata* 'Phyllis Craig' is a small-leaved dwarf, bushier than the parent. In California weeping fig (*F. benjamina*, page 107) in very small sizes is also used as a shrub.

RELOCATION: An ornately patterned urn best sets off the bold foliage of the fiddleleaf fig, but it looks well in round, glazed, deep-colored pottery and great in a heavy, black, sculptured iron urn. Feature this plant alone under a spotlight against a bare white wall, or pair it with a taller India rubber plant (*Ficus elastica*, page 79) or with a whole collection of ficus: a big weeping fig (*F. benjamina*, page 107), a shrub-size India rubber plant (*F. elastica*, page 79), and a low pot of creeping fig (*F. pumila*, page 130).

SITUATIONS WANTED: The fiddleleaf fig is from tropical West Africa and can take a lot of heat, to 80 or 85 degrees, as long as the soil is kept moist. Low temperatures, down to 65 degrees, are okay, too. Bright light a few feet from a big east or west window, filtered light from a south window, or right in a north window are all good. If the leaves begin to yellow and new foliage seems small compared to earlier growth, increase the light with a spot or a flood. The ficuses tend to drop leaves when acclimatizing, so be patient and experiment.

SALARY REQUIREMENTS: Keep the soil evenly moist but not soaking wet. Add water until excess appears in the saucer, but remove the excess an hour after watering. Dry soil results in falling leaves. Mist and air the plant as often as you can, especially when it's first adjusting to the office, and sponge the leaves clean monthly. Feed all-purpose plant food at half the amount recommended on the package. Top dress large plants as needed with all-purpose soil. If you need to repot, use all-purpose soil over 2 inches of gravel to guarantee adequate drainage.

FYI: Poor light or dry or soggy soil cause leaf drop.

Pandanus veitchii
SCREW PINE

RESUMÉ: A young screw pine looks like the rosette of a green and white striped dracaena. In its native Polynesia, the rosettes of sword-shaped, creamy-margined leaves grow at the ends of branches and the tops of thick round straight-up trunks. They're remarkably different from vegetation on this continent and unlike anything we call a pine tree. Young plants of this long-lived species will grow to 6 feet indoors and with age develop sticklike aerial roots. There's an attractive dwarf, *Pandanus veitchii compactus*, that is variegated white and stays small. The screw pine is a dramatic and durable office plant.

RELOCATION: Young screw pines look marvelous in deep blue or red glazed ceramic containers, but they also look great in severe white plastic cylinders. The plant is dramatic enough to be worth featuring alone, but it groups well with other types that thrive under fluorescents and grow lights, like Chinese evergreens (*Aglaonema*, page 26), cathedral windows (*Calathea makoyana*, page 35), and small-leaved philodendrons.

SITUATIONS WANTED: Screw pine can take high temperatures to 80 degrees but will do better if the temperature is cooler than that. Lows to 65 degrees at night are all right. Light should be moderate: a few feet from an east or west window, right in a north window, or several feet from a curtained south window. Grow lights and fluorescents directly overhead are fine, too. The less light there is, the less the creamy white of the margins.

SALARY REQUIREMENTS: Frequent watering in summer is the rule, but in winter let the plant rest by allowing the soil to dry out a little between waterings. When the top layer of soil is without moisture, drench the plant until excess seeps into the saucer, wait an hour, and then empty the saucer. Mist often in winter, and sponge the leaves clean monthly. Feed all-purpose plant food half as often as recommended. If the roots become crowded, repot in all-purpose soil; use all-purpose soil to top dress plants too large to repot.

FYI: Red spider mites will attack screw pine when air is dry.

Philodendron selloum
CUT- OR SPLIT-LEAVED PHILODENDRON

RESUMÉ: *Philodendron selloum* has great big round, deep-cut leaves up to 2 feet wide and resembles *Monstera deliciosa* (also known as P. pertusum). *P. selloum* is one of the philodendron types called self-heading vines, which grow on tree trunks. Young plants usually are sold staked to half logs of bark; if yours isn't, best add a stake. In their native tropical setting, the philodendrons are spectacular plants; here, because they'll take neglect without dying, they rarely get the kind of tender loving care that produces magnificence. A pity, because a mature thriving *P. selloum* is a remarkable plant, a great, lush spill that says jungle all over.

RELOCATION: A big plant looks wonderful in a busily patterned ceramic jar or in any kind of simple wicker, cane, or rope cachepot. A large *P. selloum* is enough of an attention getter to place in the reception area, a corridor, or a small office. It furnishes a small space completely. To make the most of it, stand it on a pedestal or atop a file cabinet.

SITUATIONS WANTED: Philodendrons can stand heat into the 80s; low at night can be to 65 degrees. They need light (a little direct sun) and do best near an east or west window or right in a bright north window. Young plants grow well under fluorescents, but big plants may need a spot, too.

SALARY REQUIREMENTS: This is a plant that thrives on moisture. It can take neglect, but if you want it to look gorgeous, keep the soil evenly moist. Water until the saucer fills; an hour later, remove the excess. Mist daily if temperatures are high, and sponge leaves clean monthly. If the plant grows too quickly, you can cut it back and it will bush out and grow even more beautiful. Feed all-purpose plant food half as often as directed on container. Keep the plant slightly pot-bound; it seems to grow better that way. Repot in all-purpose soil over 2 inches of drainage pebbles only if growth is checking. Top dress big plants annually.

FYI: Cold temperatures and bone-dry hot air can spoil the plant. Red spider mites attack in dry heats.

Phoenix roebelenii
PIGMY DATE PALM

RESUMÉ: This regal little shrub belongs to the feathery date palm group. It is a slender plant with soft, graceful drooping branches growing from several stems. It's one of the best palms for offices, being showy, durable, beautiful, and reaching to about 12 feet in good conditions. A young plant grows a quite symmetrical rosette of feathery leaves; when the plant gets to be 12 feet, it has developed a slender trunk topped by a round thick crown of very graceful fronds.

RELOCATION: The symmetry of the pigmy date palm makes it quite formal. It's equally complemented by a white plastic cylinder, a cement urn, a terracotta pot, or a glazed ceramic cachepot. Place a young plant on a pedestal to increase its height; it needs room all around, so it must have a central position. Several very young plants are charming in a row in a high planter—a delightful room divider. When you place the pigmy date palm, be wary of landing it in a dead-air corner—it needs fresh air.

SITUATIONS WANTED: The pigmy date palm does best in moderate to warm temperatures; up to 80 degrees during the day and as low as 65 degrees at night are okay. Most suitable light is near a bright east or west window or several feet from a venetian-blinded south window. Often, the palms will adapt to light right under overhead fluorescents; if they aren't doing well in eight hours of fluorescents, burn the lights for another four hours after the staff leaves. A timer can turn them off. Or add a spotlight during the day to increase the footcandles.

SALARY REQUIREMENTS: Keep the soil evenly moist. Don't ever let it dry out. Yellow fronds and brown leaf tips are the penalty, and the damaged areas can only be cut away. Use scissors since the dead tips won't pull off without tearing the plant. Mist date palm daily, and air the room often if temperatures are high. Feed all-purpose plant food half as often as package recommends. When roots fill the pot, repot in three parts all-purpose soil and one part peat. Place 2 inches of pebbles in the pot bottom for drainage. Top dress big plants annually with all-purpose soil. Sponge fronds clean several times a year.

FYI: Beware of mealybugs and scale.

Pittosporum tobira
JAPANESE PITTOSPORUM

RESUMÉ: This is a broadleaf evergreen that will remind you of that popular indoor plant Schefflera (*Brassaia actinophylla*, page 100). The leaves are bright green, leathery long ovals, and grow in a whorl at the ends of long stems. There's a beautiful variegated sort whose leaves have silvery margins. A healthy plant produces small fragrant white flowers and grows to 10 feet tall. Pittosporum is a durable, long-lasting office shrub.

RELOCATION: Pittosporum looks wonderful in a busily patterned cachepot—a Chinese or Indian ceramic, for instance. When the plant gets taller, it looks best in a dim white plastic cylinder. Young plants are imposing enough to dress the reception area and great as a background plant in a grouping that includes linears such as false aralia (*Dizygotheca elegantissima*, page 75), *Polyscias fruticosa* (page 86), or with mature ferns.

SITUATIONS WANTED: Cool is the key here; pittosporum does not enjoy hot places. Day temperatures between 60 and 70 degress are best, and at night they can go down to 50 degrees. As the plant grows taller, reaching into the hotter air of the office stratosphere, new growth may suffer, so mist and air the plants often. Light can be full sun a few feet from a south window, right in an east or west window, or in a north window augmented by fluorescent, spots, floods. My own pittosporum does well placed right under a bank of 40-watt fluorescents; you can add a spotlight if yours looks peaked.

SALARY REQUIREMENTS: Allow the topsoil to become moderately dry before you water, then water till the saucer fills. An hour later, empty excess water. During summer and fall, feed all-purpose plant food half as often as package directs. Switch to blooming-type plant food winter and spring, again feeding half as often as directed. When the plant dwarfs the container, repot in all-purpose soil over 2 inches of drainage pebbles; top dress big plants annually with all-purpose soil. Sponge the leaves a few times a year.

FYI: Hot blasts will shrivel new growth; red spider mites attack if you don't mist in temperatures over 68 degrees.

Podocarpus macrophylla maki
SOUTHERN YEW

RESUMÉ: This plant is called southern yew in the south, where it is used as a hedge plant. Another name for it is Buddhist pine, which has an exotic ring more suggestive of the look of the plant. It is from China, a narrow-leaved evergreen that may remind you of the foliage in ancient Chinese scroll paintings. As long as you can keep it cool, it's a great office plant that in time will reach for the ceiling.

RELOCATION: As a young plant, southern yew is a small, elegant subject ideally set off by a beautifully patterned oriental urn. Or you can go the other way and set it off in a neat white cylinder. It is also magnificent in one of those expensive polished aluminum cubes. Young plants are best displayed in a group; their delicate needling makes a nice contrast next to bold-leafed plants such as *Philodendron selloum* (page 82) and the fiddleleaf fig (*Ficus lyrata*, page 80). A big podocarpus is striking and should be featured alone against a stark wall or on a pedestal in a reception area. Add spotlights to dramatize its beauty; it can probably use some extra footcandles of light.

SITUATIONS WANTED: Podocarpus needs cool to moderate temperatures: Between 60 and 70 degrees during the day is best, with lows to 50 degrees at night. Light should be between bright and filtered: a few feet from a curtained sunny south window; near an east or west window; or right in a very bright north window, especially if fluorescent light spills around the area. This is a plant that needs air, so don't set it in a corner.

SALARY REQUIREMENTS: Keep the soil evenly moist but not soggy, especially if light is on the low side. Don't let excess water stay in the saucer for more than an hour. Mist daily if the temperature is over 70 degrees, and air as often as you can. Feed all-purpose plant food half as often as the package directs. Top dress large plants annually with three parts all-purpose soil and one part peat. If necessary, repot, including 2 inches of pebbles in the bottom for drainage. When podocarpus gets tall, it may grow better if it is staked.

FYI: Red spider mites are a hazard if temperatures are over 70 degrees. Blasts of hot dry air will spoil the leaves.

Polyscias fruticosa 'Elegans'
PARSLEY ARALIA

RESUMÉ: *Polyscias fruticosa* 'Elegans' is a dense, elegant little evergreen shrub that comes from Polynesia. The feathery cut and curl of the leathery leaves are the reason for the common name, parsley aralia. It's very desirable and rather expensive. There are some other polyscias grown indoors—taller sorts you might like to look at in shrub sizes. *P. fruticosa* strings itself out more than *P. f.* 'Elegans.' In the next chapter, two large species are suggested for tree use: *P. balfouriana* and *P. filicifolia* (pages 111–112), often referred to as Ming tree. They all look oriental. Suppliers offer shrub sizes, 12 to 18 inches tall, at reasonable prices.

RELOCATION: Anything so obviously oriental looks good in a Chinese urn or a big bonsai dish. Use a young plant in a small reception area. It looks elegant grouped with plants of unusual shapes, like a big basket of rosary vine (*Ceropegia woodii*, page 128) or tree-size *P. filicifolia*.

SITUATIONS WANTED: Polyscias enjoy a broad temperature range—up to 80 or even 85 degrees on occasion, if there's air moving around, and down to 65 degrees. They need moisture and good light. A few feet from a bright east or west window or right in a north window will maintain the shrub, but if you want it to grow, try it in a position that provides several hours of direct light daily. New plants adapt to less light, though they may need months to acclimate; bright overhead fluorescents may be enough light as long as there is some light from nearby windows. It may yellow leaves in the beginning, but the plant is pretty durable—as long as you don't keep shifting its position.

SALARY REQUIREMENTS: Keep the soil evenly moist; don't let it dry out. Don't let excess water stay in the saucer for more than an hour. Try to mist daily when temperatures are high and air is dry. Feed all-purpose plant food half as often as package directs, less if light is low. Repot only if container becomes crowded; top dress large plants once a year, using all-purpose soil. Sponge leaves once or twice a year to keep the plant beautiful.

FYI: Red spider mites attack in dry heat; so mist often.

Rhapis excelsa
LADY PALM

RESUMÉ: This is a miniature palm with several reedy stems and rather broad leaves growing in a fan shape. It eventually reaches 10 or 12 feet and is a popular indoor plant in the East. There are several kinds: *Rhapis excelsa* is called the large lady palm; *R. e.* 'Variegata,' from Japan, has white-striped leaves; and *R. humilis*, which you can find in California in small sizes, is called the slender lady palm and grows only to 4 feet. The broad foliage of the fan palm grows up more than out and makes a bolder pattern than that of palms such as the date palm (*Phoenix roebelenii*). It's more graceful than the kentia palm (*Howeia fosteriana*) but a little less tough, perhaps.

RELOCATION: Several young plants can be used to fill a planter or set on file cabinets; they will serve as graceful area dividers. Lady palm—especially a large one—is lovely alone on a pedestal. Or pair it with the big bold foliage of *Philodendron selloum* (page 82); they balance each other.

SITUATIONS WANTED: The temperatures comfortable for you suit rhapis: 70-degree days with nights as low as 55 degrees. But rhapis must have air; don't abandon it to an airless corner. The best light is near an east or west window or a few feet from a curtained south window. Overhead fluorescents with some sun from nearby windows are good, too. But ordinary fluorescents alone may be enough to keep this palm happy if all other conditions are right.

SALARY REQUIREMENTS: Keep the soil evenly moist; never let it dry out. However, don't let it stay soggy after watering, either; empty saucer excess at the end of an hour. Mist daily if temperatures are over 70 degrees and sponge clean the leaves of young plants several times a year. Feed all-purpose plant food half as often as package directs. Repot if the plant begins to look top-heavy; the roots of the plant may be outgrowing the pot, too. Top dress big plants annually with three parts all-purpose soil and one part peat. Use scissors to cut away browned frond edges or yellowed fronds.

FYI: Hot or icy drafts spoil the plant. Red spider mites will attack in hot, dry stale air.

4
Office Trees

If you want a tree for free, turn to page 109 and grow your own avocado (*Persea americana*). If, on the other hand, you're after an instant tree, welcome to Chapter 4.

When is a plant a tree? If it has a single stem that branches, it is probably a tree. For our purposes, it's a tree when you have to raise your eyes to see the top. Say, 8 feet.

About 90 percent of new construction in the Northeast has 8-foot ceilings. And up to 8 feet, tree-size plants remain within a reasonable price range, but over 8 feet the price jumps. That is because tractor trailers from Florida (the source of much of our plant material) have 8-foot ceilings. Taller trees must be laid down flat for their travels. Since shipping is priced on a per-square-foot basis and nothing can be piled on top of a flat-out tree, shipping charges jump drastically over 8 feet. So—settle for 8-foot trees, unless you have a lot of money to spend, a terribly high ceiling, or no patience. As I've said many times before, young plants acclimate more easily than mature plants, making the young ones the safest and best (and most fun) investment.

Most of the trees described in this chapter cost between $10 and $15 per linear foot; an 8-foot tree might cost from $80 to $120. Some cost even more; a tree-size *Polyscias filicifolia* can cost hundreds of dollars.

Big trees require roomy containers. Baskets in which to hide the pots start at $10 and go up; a polished aluminum container for a tree ranges at around $100. The other types—plastic, china, pottery, terracotta—cost something in between.

1 *Dracaena marginata;* **2** *Chamaedorea seifritzii;* **3** *Persea americana*

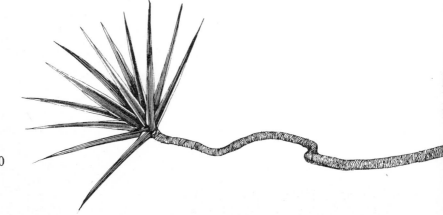

Since plants in the tree and shrub categories cross lines according to age, the basic information on shrubs in Chapter 3 applies to trees as well: Guides on buying, containers, climate, light, watering, feeding, are similar for both trees and shrubs. There are only a few thoughts to add.

Lighting

A tree is a real investment; guard the investment by spending the money to put in recessed ceiling spots if you doubt there's enough light. Floodlights or spots on extendable stands might do as well and will serve to dramatize the plant. Management is usually most willing to buy a tree for the reception area, and that, in my experience, is often the place that has the least window light. If a ceiling spot or a floor flood is a problem during the day, it can be turned on when you leave; most plants don't keep office hours.

Watering

There is no possibility of lifting a tree-size plant to empty its saucer, so follow suggestions on pages 68–69 for ways to gauge the right amount of water for each plant. Be particularly careful not to let pot bottoms of plants that like to be evenly or quite moist —the clustered fishtail palm for instance—sit for days in puddles. They simply can't stand it.

Be especially wary on this score of big plants in tall tubs. I usually can't see the bottoms of mine to tell whether water has collected there or not. More than once I've removed a ruined schefflera to find it had been living in stagnant water inches deep. Double-check when the cachepot is tall: A tall stick will tell you if there's water there.

Trees that do best when the soil is evenly moist benefit from mulching. A thin layer of pretty river-washed pebbles or chunks of wood moss (not one big sheet that blocks air) are attractive mulches that do the job. Or, use small vining plants or low ferns.

Feeding

The information in Chapter 3 about feeding shrubs applies to trees. Since you don't often repot plants this size, you should top dress them annually.

Top dressing is a simple but messy job. Some night when everybody has gone home, spread many thicknesses of newspaper over the floor around the plant. With a small digging tool or a big spoon or a ruler, gently loosen the top 2 inches of soil all around the main stem of the plant. Scoop the soil into a pail on the newspaper. Replace the soil with loosely packed potting soil of whatever kind is suggested for that particular plant, mixed with sand or humus or any additives needed. Commercial potting soil usually has plant food mixed into it, so don't add ferti-

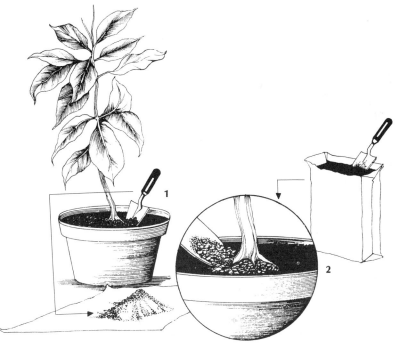

TOP DRESSING: **1** Remove an inch of old topsoil. **2** Replace with a rich mixture of fresh top-soil.

ROOT PRUNING: *Ficus elastica*

lizer. Water the plant well after you've patted the soil into place. And that's all there is to top dressing; except, you have to clean up the papers and get the dirt out from under your nails.

Root pruning, illustrated here, is another way to handle big plants that outgrow their potting soil. Cut the small outside roots as shown, fill the original container with fresh soil, and repot.

Every three or four years, trees should be repotted. You repot a tree the same way you repot an African violet, but it's harder, heavier work, which is described more fully in Chapter 8.

Decorating

Trees make a strong statement. They put foliage up in the air in a big way. They need space to be effective, or they become oppressive. If you don't like the tree you are living with, check the size of the room. It takes a room at least 15 feet by 20 feet to show off a round-headed 6-foot tree. By the time that tree is 8 feet tall, the room may seem crowded. The generalization holds in its multiples: Two 6-foot trees need a room 30 by 40 feet, etc. There are, of course, exceptions to this, as to all other rules.

In an office 20 by 28 feet, you can fit a small floor garden that includes a tree—if it's a tidy garden and a fairly trim tree, like an 8-foot bamboo palm (*Chamaedorea erumpens*), but it takes an entire large lobby to accommodate and show off a mature areca palm (*Chrysalidocarpus lutescens*). If you don't have room for trees, don't buy them. There are alternatives with which you might satisfy yourself. For instance, you can get a tree effect that looks good in a small space by putting a narrow plant, like a 3- or 4-foot *Dracaena marginata*, on a low file cabinet; and a tall skinny corn plant (*Dracaena fragrans*, page 106) can suit a room less than 15 feet by 20 feet.

Before you choose a given tree, go have a look at the real thing; a picture in a catalog doesn't tell the whole story.

FLOOR GARDENS

A tree-centered floor garden is a good investment for a large workroom; it can be absolutely beautiful. Suggestions for floor-garden plants are included in this chapter within the individual discussions under the headings Relocation.

A floor garden is easiest to care for if the pots are all set on one big tin-lined tray holding pebbles 2 inches deep. The moist pebbles create a microclimate that helps eliminate the threat of red spider mites. Even desert plants like yucca enjoy the moisture. And the tray makes watering easy for the sloppiest maintenance crew, since the tray catches seepage and spills.

One caution about planning gardens: Light reaches plants from windows and overhead fluorescents unevenly. So, think of each plant's needs before you assign it to your garden. Trees and shrubs on pedestals get light from many sources, as I said before, but plants on the floor may be cut off from window light and are far from overhead fluorescents. Spotlights add drama as well as footcandles to a floor garden and can solve such light problems.

When I am choosing plants for a floor garden, I select a tree first, then shrubs, then table-size and basket plants that will heighten the effect of the tree. The little tree called 'Song of India' (*Pleomele reflexa variegata*) is a beautifully dense-leaved plant whose foliage is streaked with white. To set it off, I have listed with it several smaller plants that also have variegated foliage but contrasting leaf shape and branch structure; the effect is dynamite—really dramatic.

Another way of going about the floor garden is to choose smaller plants whose foliage contrasts sharply with the tree foliage. The foliage of *Philodendron selloum* (page 82) is huge and deeply cut. It has a jungle look that is a great contrast for the feathery airy parlor and fan palms. The jade plant has thick jewel-green little leaves that complement but contrast sharply with the cut-out lacy green of the exotic and dramatic *Polyscias filicifolia*.

Once I've found foliage and heights that make good combinations, I make sure the plants can thrive—or at least survive—happily in the same climate: hot, cold, bright light or filtered are the main concerns. Ponder before you discard a favorite from your garden design, though. Plants are adaptable. If it's cool in the room at your level, it may be of suitable warmth up there where the treetop lives. If it is dim at your level, it may be brighter near the ceiling.

Selection

The plants on the following pages are among the toughest as well as the most generally available of the various tree sizes that live indoors. There are a lot of palms, because tropicals can live with you. There is also a real needled pine, Norfolk Island pine (*Araucaria excelsa*) ; a round-headed tree like those on your lawn, the weeping fig (*Ficus benjamina* 'Exotica') ; a desert tree, spineless yucca (*Yucca elephantipes*) ; as well as a handful of fascinating hard-to-describe exotics. In other words, there's enough variety to create almost any decorative effect you may have in mind.

In California, Florida, and other points south, you will probably find available in tree sizes neanthe bella palm, (which is *Chamaedorea elegans* 'Bella' in Chapter 3) ; large sizes of *Ficus retusa nitida*; and large sizes of other plants the rest of us usually can find only in shrub sizes. You will also find in the south a wider selection of tree palms.

On the other hand, in warm regions you may not find some of the plants we have which require bright light. Southern architects put effort into keeping sun out of buildings to save on air-conditioning costs. Among tree sizes hard to find in warmer regions are *Ficus benjamina* 'Exotica,' *Pleomele reflexa,* the polyscias, and *Veitchia merrillii,* which is the Manila palm.

Trees that are good indoors if you can supply some summer outdoors include, along with the citrus plants suggested in Chapter 3, the kumquat (*Fortunella margarita*) and the tamarind (*Tamarindus indica*).

The Plants

Araucaria excelsa
NORFOLK ISLAND PINE

RESUMÉ: This is a real pine tree from an island in the South Pacific belonging to Australia. In its homeland, it soars up to 200 feet; potted, young plants the size of shrubs grow up very slowly to become office trees. The foliage of the young plants looks soft; the branches are widely spaced and formal in their symmetry. There is some confusion about the name: It is also known as Araucaria heterophylla.

RELOCATION: The smaller the container, the less the plant will grow; if you buy a young plant and want it to grow big, repot it as often as the roots become crowded, using inexpensive containers. If you want it to stay small, keep it underpotted. Place a 3- to 4-foot plant on a pedestal; it make a tree-size plant suitable for a reception area. Norfolk Island pine is attractive in a floor garden including *Fatsia japonica* (page 78), with an overgrown grape ivy (page 129) on a low pedestal, like a plastic cube, for instance, in white or red.

SITUATIONS WANTED: Best temperatures are on the cool side; 65 degrees is great; 70 degrees is okay during the day, as long as there is fresh air. Don't let this plant sit near hot drafts. Best light is near an east or west window, right in a bright north window, or under fluorescents augmented by window light or 150-watt spots. A few hours of direct sun daily will help young plants to grow quickly.

SALARY REQUIREMENTS: Water often enough to keep the soil evenly moist; if it dries out, needles will drop and won't be replaced. In winter Monday and Thursday watering might be better than a once-a-week drenching. Don't leave excess water in the pot. Mist often—daily if temperatures are over 70 degrees. Feed all-purpose plant food half as often as package directs. When roots crowd container, repot in three parts all-purpose soil and one part peat. Use this mix to top dress plants that are too big to repot. If the tree hits the ceiling, cut off the top foot or two and root it in moist soil to start a new tree.

FYI: Red spider attacks in dry heat.

1 *Brassaia actinophylla;* 2 *Scindapsus aureus;* 3 *Philodendron selloum;*
4 *Tradescantia*

Brassaia actinophylla
SCHEFFLERA
QUEENSLAND UMBRELLA TREE

RESUMÉ: This is the tree most commonly found in offices; the leaves seem to be lacquered a vibrant green, which are its big asset. Its looks are easily spoiled if its needs aren't met, so study it carefully before you invest. Young plants make good shrubs and are easier to acclimate than tree-size plants. Florists call this Schefflera actinophylla.

RELOCATION: The big leaves are graceful but informal, a sort of tumbled arrangement sometimes dense, sometimes sparse. Baskets and trim white plastic containers suit this plant best. A young plant set on a file cabinet doubles easily as a tree. A single mature plant is all a small reception area can take and makes a sound backdrop for a floor garden set several yards from a big sunny window; the garden might include: parsley aralia (*Polyscias fruticosa*, page 86) set on a tall pedestal; fiddleleaf fig (*Ficus lyrata*, page 80); *Philodendron selloum* (page 82) on the floor in a big bowl. You may add variegated pothos (*Scindapsus aureus*, page 135); a basket of wandering jew (*Tradescantia*, page 138); coleus (page 37) under a spotlight; prayer plant (*Maranta*, page 48); and little pots of African violets (*Saintpaulia*, page 162) in bloom.

SITUATIONS WANTED: Schefflera needs bright light and warmth. It can take up to 80 degrees, but hot drafts are damaging. Heat is apt to be too high and dry up near the ceiling for young growth, so a big schefflera is better off in a 70-degree office. It needs bright light but won't take hot sun close to a window; light received at a slant or a north window with additional light from fluorescents is safer. If there isn't enough light, stems grow long and droop under the weight of the leaves.

SALARY REQUIREMENTS: Wait until surface soil is rather dry before watering, then drench until water seeps into the saucer. An hour later remove remaining water. Soggy soil is a most common cause of black leaf tips. Mist often. Feed all-purpose plant food half as often as recommended, and top dress the soil annually with three parts all-purpose soil and one part peat. Clean the leaves a few times a year.

FYI: Red spider mites and soggy soil are hazardous.

Caryota mitis
CLUSTERED FISHTAIL PALM

RESUMÉ: The fishtail palm is very decorative and quite unlike the other palms in this book. The branches grow as palm branches usually do, but the "leaves" look like many-boned fishtails or fins, and they grow on the branches in a way that creates a remarkable pattern. Lots of suckers grow up from the base of potted plants, so there is green there, too. All of the various Caryota species are very forgiving plants, but *Caryota mitis* to my mind is the prettiest.

RELOCATION: I prefer this palm in an ornate ceramic urn, though it looks very much at home in any kind of woven basket and is great in Mexican pottery, too. If you want an interestingly busy leaf group for an important place or a boring wall, make a floor garden including the fishtail palm; a young false aralia (*Dizygotheca elegantissima*, page 75); an overgrown spider plant (*Chlorophytum comosum*, page 36) and on the floor place two or three pots of Chinese evergreen (*Aglaonema*, page 26) in a brightly variegated species.

SITUATIONS WANTED: Warm temperatures—up to 80 degrees—suit this palm, as they do many others, but avoid hot drafts. Night temperatures can go down to 65 degrees. Light near an east or west window or in a bright north window augmented by overhead fluorescents or several feet from a curtained south window should be sufficient. Fluorescents alone might be all right if floods and spots are added—150 watts or 100 watts if the blubs are incandescent.

SALARY REQUIREMENTS: Keep the soil quite moist. Never let caryota dry out. Water twice weekly in winter if needed. Without fail, empty the saucer of excess water an hour after watering. Mist often during winter and while the plant is new to the office. Feed all-purpose plant food half as often as package directs. Top dress the soil annually with three parts all-purpose soil and one part peat. Dust the leaves several times a year with a feather duster to keep the plant clean—you can't really sponge it.

FYI: Hot blasts of air and dry soil spoil the leaves, but over-watering can kill it.

Chamaedorea erumpens
BAMBOO PALM

Chamaedorea erumpens

RESUMÉ: The Chamaedora clan includes the little neanthe bella palm recommended as a shrub in the previous chapter. The bamboo palm is a rather informal plant recommended by decorators all the time because it is indestructible once established. It has bamboolike stalks bearing broad, papery, palm-type "leaves" curved down and appearing here and there on the plant from short and tall stalks. The species *Chamaedorea seifrizii* usually has more stalks, more slender leaves, and a lacier look. A mature plant resembles a stand of fresh bamboo growing right in the office. In California, *C. erumpens* is more often sold in shrub size. If you can find young plants and have patience, get them—they are less costly.

RELOCATION: I love these palms in big wicker baskets, but they also look great in plastic cubes and Chinese urns. A single 10-foot plant in a corner against a white wall looks marvelous. Add a small painting, say 12 by 15 inches, and a slender straight-backed chair to balance the many linears of the group, and you have a charming little vignette.

SITUATIONS WANTED: The bamboo palm likes warm temperatures to 80 or 85 degrees, moisture, and dim light. I placed a young chamaedorea beside, not in, a south window and it did nothing. Moved to a really dim corner to the left of a tightly shuttered west window, it reached the ceiling in a year or so. It got a little additional light from a window slanted toward the southwest and from very low overhead fluorescents. Dim light, I conclude, is its preference.

SALARY REQUIREMENTS: Keep the soil evenly moist, and keep the plant on moist pebbles in a big tray. Cover the top of the soil with patches of wood moss to help maintain even moisture without keeping the soil soaking wet. Mist as often as you can. Feed all-purpose plant food half as often as package directs. Annually top dress with three parts all-purpose soil and one part peat. Sponge the fronds gently two or three times a year, and help new fronds to open—they sometimes stick.

FYI: Hot or cold drafts are damaging. Red spider mites may attack in relentlessly dry heat.

Chrysalidocarpus lutescens
ARECA PALM

RESUMÉ: The areca, or butterfly, palm is probably the most graceful of all palms, exquisitely beautiful in an elegant, formal way but trickier than others to grow successfully indoors. It's a large palm, to 25 feet, with a yellow stalk and yellow-green foliage that grows right to ground level. When it is well cared for, it looks most of all like a bunch of gorgeous plumes in a clump.

RELOCATION: This palm needs a beautiful container. It can be a carefully woven basket or a magnificently ornate Chinese urn. A single tree-size areca palm will decorate a large reception area, a small lobby, or a big conference room. It can be a grand centerpiece for a round floor garden; surround it with several shrubs on pedestals at different levels. Place table-size plants in matching pots near the pedestals. Good companions are any plants that can take warm temperatures and moisture. Or, bring in florist imports on loan (see Chapter 6). Flowering seasonal plants, such as azaleas, interspersed with fuzzy ferns make a lovely display.

SITUATIONS WANTED: Warm temperatures are essential—it will take to 80 or 85 degrees, with lows at night down to 65 degrees. Areca palms like moisture, too, so mist often if there is no humidifier, especially when you first acquire the plant. Light can be from a skylight if it is bright, near an east or west window, in a bright north window, or several feet from a curtained south window. Overhead fluorescents are okay if they are augmented by some window sun or 150-watt spots. The plant adapts if there is enough humidity (see below).

SALARY REQUIREMENTS: Keep the soil quite moist. A mulch of pieces of wood moss helps. Set the plant on a bed of wet pebbles (but water level must be below the pot bottom) to increase humidity in the air. Feed all-purpose plant food half as often as package directs. Top dress the areca palm annually with three parts all-purpose soil and one part peat, and dust fronds occasionally with a feather duster.

FYI: Red spider mites attack in dry heat. Icy drafts spoil the plant. Dried-out soil kills fronds.

Chrysalidocarpus lutescens

Dracaena marginata and *D. fragrans massangeana*

RESUMÉS: Some dracaenas in shrub sizes appear in Chapter 3. The two here, *Dracaena marginata* and *D. fragrans massangeana*, are popular, decorative, striking, and durable office trees. *D. f. massangeana* looks like the common corn plant but has slender, yellow-striped, cornlike leaves climbing the slender stalk. Mature *D. marginata* has several slender trunks (stems) that look like miniature palm trunks. They're weird but wonderful.

RELOCATION: *D. marginata* is an attention getter, whatever the container. Although *D. f. massangeana* looks great in baskets or in oriental pottery, I prefer it in tall slender cylinders or rectangular containers. *D. marginata* is so striking it can be used alone in a small lobby, a reception area, or the conference room with perhaps a jade plant (*Crassula argentea*, pages 38–39) a few feet away in a matching container. *D. f. massangeana* is the perfect tall plant to back a small floor garden including the fiddleleaf fig (*Ficus lyrata*, page 80), small philodendrons (page 134), Chinese evergreens (*Aglaonema*, page 26), and pots of white flag (*Spathiphyllum*, page 163).

SITUATIONS WANTED: The dracaenas can take daytime temperatures to 80 or 85 degrees, nights to 65 degrees, and adapt fairly easily to almost any situation. Best light is near an east or west window, in a bright north window, or near a venetian-blinded south window. They'll also do well under office fluorescents. I am growing *D. marginata* on a low file cabinet under very low overhead incandescents, with a little light from a west window, and *D. massangeana* under a 75-watt spot.

SALARY REQUIREMENTS: Keep the soil quite moist but not soggy. If the soil dries out, leaf tips will brown. Water till excess pours into saucer; empty the saucer an hour later. Mist often. Sponge the leaves clean a few times yearly. If leaf tips brown, trim spoiled areas with scissors. Feed all-purpose plant food half as often as package directs. Top dress big plants annually with all-purpose soil.

FYI: *D. marginata* is subject to red spider mites.

Ficus benjamina
WEEPING FIG

RESUMÉ: This is my favorite of all office trees, a real tree-type tree, slender trunked with a big head of weeping, willowy branches covered with small, long-tipped oval leaves. It looks a little like a miniature weeping aspen. Two kinds are commonly offered: *Ficus benjamina*, the one Californians find most easily, has drooping branches, and *F. b.* 'Exotica,' called Java fig, is especially graceful. Either one is gorgeous. Weeping figs are sold in sizes ranging from 3 to 15 feet. They grow reasonably quickly, are expensive, and lose leaves and branches while acclimating; for all those reasons, the smaller, cheaper sizes are the best investment.

RELOCATION: A weeping fig looks great in any container, even the green tub it comes in, so choose a pot that suits your office decor. If you've bought a young plant, raise it to quick tree status by placing it on a pedestal. For a large conference room, group three weeping figs of different heights in a row, smallest to tallest. When the biggest gets too big, replace it with a young tree and promote the big tree to another floor or the executive suite.

SITUATIONS WANTED: Weeping figs prefer to be a little cool and need lots of fresh air and light. They'll take direct sun late in the day; or place yours in an east or west window, a north window augmented by fluorescents, or fluorescents augmented by some daily sunlight. They drop lots of leaves while acclimatizing; when my favorite was moved from a cool, airy country house to a hot stuffy office, it dropped leaves for eight months until it looked like a plucked chicken—but it survived.

SALARY REQUIREMENTS: Keep the soil evenly moist but not soggy. Water till excess pours into the saucer; remove the excess after an hour. Cover soil with pebbles or small clay pots of tiny creeping fig (*Ficus pumila*, page 130). Mist daily if you can, especially when first purchased, and air often. Feed all-purpose plant food at half strength as often as directions suggest and top dress annually with all-purpose soil. Remove dead twigs and dust or sponge the leaves as often as you have the patience.

FYI: Red spider mites attack in hot airless rooms.

Howeia fosteriana
KENTIA PALM

RESUMÉ: *Howeia fosteriana* is a tall elegant tree, sometimes called the paradise palm, that you'll see in the florist shops because indoors it is the most durable of all the big palms. It has graceful big fronds, those at the top being larger than those low down. The leaves are waxy and a deep green. Outdoors the kentia palm grows to 50 feet; indoors it goes right to the ceiling in a few years. In California small sizes are sold as shrubs more cheaply than full-grown trees.

RELOCATION: The kentia palm is a little less formal than the date palm (*Phoenix roebelenii*) and undemanding when it comes to a container. Mexican pottery or terracotta suits it well. Actually, it looks pretty good in the original green tub! It's a good choice for a lobby, reception area, or conference room and interesting as the centerpiece for a group of smaller palms such as the European fan palm (*Chamaerops humilis*, page 72) or the sago palm (*Cycas revoluta*, page 73), for instance. I also like it with a massive pot of *Philodendron selloum* (page 82) nearby; that kind of philodendron has an overgrown tropical look I like with palms, especially if there are big ferns to add to the group—and flowers, too.

SITUATIONS WANTED: The kentia palm adapts fairly easily to less than ideal conditions. Its basic needs are for moderate temperatures and light. It prefers 70 degrees in the day and can take down to 55 degrees at night. Best light is near an east or west window, right in a north window, or several feet from a curtained south window. Overhead fluorescents augmented by strong window light, such as described, should be fine.

SALARY REQUIREMENTS: Keep the soil evenly moist. A mossy mulch is a help and decorative as well. Water thoroughly every week or ten days until water seeps into saucer; an hour later empty the saucer. Mist often and air if temperatures are over 70 degrees. Feed all-purpose plant food half as often as package recommends. Top dress annually with three parts all-purpose soil and one part peat. Dust occasionally.

FYI: Red spider mites attack in hot, dry rooms. Mist often to avoid them.

Persea americana
AVOCADO TREE

RESUMÉ: This tree costs nothing but the price of four avocados, which you can justify by making a salad. The stem is slender and willowy; the leaves very large, oval, and rather long. Kept pruned back for its first months, even years, an avocado will grow into a ceiling-high tree in almost any shape you like; you control the shape by pinching out branch tips as they grow. If the tree can spend the summer outdoors in a slightly shaded spot, it will grow much faster. (See below for instructions on growing an avocado tree.)

RELOCATION: An avocado tree looks great in a basket or a trim plastic white tub. It complements a small office, or raised on a pedestal, it attracts attention in a larger room. I think it looks nicest with a lot of ferns on pedestals of different heights in a small office garden, but I've seen it trained almost like a creeper up and around window frames or up to the ceiling and then out as far as the branches will go, which is far.

SITUATIONS WANTED: The avocado needs cool air and filtered but bright light—an east or west window, coupled with fluorescents. In less light the stem grows very tall and spindly. Cool air means temperatures around 70 or 72 degrees during the day, low to 55 degrees at night.

TO GROW AN AVOCADO TREE: In an 8-inch pot set in a saucer full of moist pebbles, bury four clean pits, broad ends down, so the tips just show above the soil. Keep the pot in a warm place with filtered or dim light until the pits sprout, then move to an east or west window. When the stems are 8 inches tall, cut them back (be ruthless) to 4 inches. Unless you prune the tree very carefully into a formal shape, it's apt to straggle.

SALARY REQUIREMENTS: Keep the soil evenly moist and mist very often. Don't let the plant sit in stagnant puddles; empty the saucer one hour after watering. To shape the plant, prune the lead tips and branches back by pinching out new tip growth. Feed all-purpose plant food. Repot as needed in all-purpose soil. When it reaches tree size, top dress annually instead of repotting.

FYI: Red spider mites are the avocado's main enemy. To avoid them, mist often, especially in the middle of winter.

Pleomele reflexa variegata 'Song of India'

RESUMÉ: A showy little evergreen tree from India, this is a plant we used to see all the time at airports, probably because it can stand drafts and neglect. The leaves, short and narrow, cluster in dense rosettes on willowy branching stems that grow straight up from the pot. They are a deep glossy green in the species *Pleomele reflexa,* but in 'Song of India' (*P. r. variegata*), the leaves are edged with golden yellow or cream. It grows slowly to about 10 feet tall and is a gorgeous and very durable office plant.

RELOCATION: 'Song of India' is showy, and it calls for a showy container—a shiny china pot in a lovely blue or golden yellow, for instance. Shiny plastic cubes in bright reds, deep green, or white also suit it. Feature 'Song of India' as the centerpiece in a group of plants with variegated leaves: spider plant (*Chlorophytum comosum,* page 36) cascading from a pedestal; Swedish ivy (*Plectranthus,* page 53), in a variegated form; variegated *Fatsia japonica* (page 78); a silver rex begonia (page 32); variegated sansevieria (page 56); aloe (page 27); agave (page 25); geranium (page 158); or English ivy (*Hedera helix,* page 131).

SITUATIONS WANTED: 'Song of India' likes warm temperatures and strong but filtered light. Temperatures can be toward 80 degrees with a low of 65 or 60 degrees at night. Light from an east or west window or a position right in a bright north window are fine. A location with fluorescents augmented by some direct sun from a window is good. Or try strong fluorescents overhead, and if the plant doesn't respond with signs of growth in a few weeks, add spots or floods. It's a very adaptable plant.

SALARY REQUIREMENTS: Pleomele can stand neglect, but to have a beautiful plant, you must keep the soil quite moist all the time. *Not soggy.* Dry soil will brown leaf tips, but the plant hates boggy conditions. Empty saucer water an hour after watering. Mist as often as you can and air the plant if heat is high. Feed all-purpose plant food half as often as package suggests. Top dress yearly with all-purpose soil. Sponge the leaves a few times a year.

FYI: Direct hot sun for prolonged periods burns the leaves.

Polyscias balfouriana and *P. filicifolia*

RESUMÉS: The two polyscias described here are very good office evergreens, but they are distinctly different in looks. *Polyscias balfouriana* has bold rounded leathery leaves, varie-

Polyscias filicifolia

gated in the kinds called *P. b. marginata* and *P. b. pennockii.* *P. filicifolia*, like the shrub parsley aralia (*P. fruiticosa*), which has cut-out leaves, is airy as a fern, is commonly called Ming tree, and is costly. It always reminds me of the trees in the ancient Chinese scroll painting called *Summer Mountains.*

RELOCATION: I prefer *P. balfouriana* in big, heavy, bold-colored containers; however, *P. filicifolia* looks best in ornate Chinese urns, high-gloss ceramics, or big bonsai containers. Raise young plants of either sort on pedestals or file cabinets to get a quick tree effect. Spots add drama to either of these polyscias, and I don't think either needs much assistance from other plants— they stand out well alone. However, *P. filicifolia* seems a natural companion to the jade plant (*Crassula argentea*, pages 38–39) and probably looks well with *Spathiphyllum clevelandii* (page 163), too. Parsley aralia (mentioned above) also would make an interesting companion.

SITUATIONS WANTED: High humidity, air, and bright light, but no direct sun, help these plants to thrive. Fluorescents combined with light from windows bright all day should be enough. Temperatures can go as high as 80 degrees during the day, as long as there is air and moisture, and as low as 65 degrees at night. In closed, stuffy quarters, polyscias lose branches and visibly sulk. Be patient while they adjust; if you move polyscias too often, they may slowly give up the ghost.

SALARY REQUIREMENTS: Keep the soil evenly moist but not soggy. Remove excess water from the saucer one hour after watering. Mulch the soil to retain humidity. Mist daily when the plant is new. Air as often as possible. Feed all-purpose plant food half as often as directed. Top dress the plant annually with three parts all-purpose soil and one part peat added. Sponge the leaves clean several times a year.

FYI: Red spider mites will attack the polyscias in hot dry air.

Veitchia merrillii
MANILA PALM

RESUMÉ: A tall single-stemmed straight-up plant from the Philippines, Manila palm has a feathery crown of big leaves, each 5 feet long or more when it grows outdoors. Indoors, even at tree size, it looks like a charming little miniature of the palms you dream of on South Pacific islands. It formerly was classed as Adonidia merrillii and sometimes is called Christmas palm, so you may know it by another name.

RELOCATION: This big, symmetrical plant has a rather formal look, which is enhanced by a big square modern container or a heavy wicker basket. Since it really looks like a big palm when seen at a distance, it can be featured in a large formal room. It's fun to center it in a group of obviously tropical plants. Under its spreading fronds, you can raise on pedestals the exotics proposed for the corner floor garden, pages 180–182, and schefflera (*Brassaia actinophylla,* page 100).

SITUATIONS WANTED: Warmth, humidity, and diffuse sunlight fill the needs of this big palm. Temperatures can be to 80 degrees in the day and at night down to 65 degrees. Light from an east, west, or very bright north window is okay, so is light several feet from a curtained south window. In summer you may have to move the palm back several feet from a south window. Overhead fluorescents augmented by several hours of sunlight from a distant window should be okay. It will do best set on a bed of moist pebbles. Keep the water level below the pot bottom.

SALARY REQUIREMENTS: Keep the soil quite moist. Don't ever let it dry out, but don't let it get soggy, either. Remove water from the saucer an hour after watering. Mist as often as possible during the heating season. If you are growing a whole group of tropicals requiring warmth and moisture, you probably will find an electric humidifier a good investment. Feed all-purpose plant food half as often as package suggests. Top dress annually with all-purpose soil. Sponge the leaves clean a few times a year if you can.

FYI: Red spider mites attack in hot dry air. Blasts of hot air from heat convectors are damaging.

Yucca elephantipes
SPINELESS YUCCA

RESUMÉ: Young yucca looks like a rosette of swords; tree-size yucca looks like a rosette of broad swords growing on the branching trunk of a palm tree. Outdoors it grows rapidly to about 30 feet tall and in spring produces a big head of creamy flowers. It isn't likely to bloom indoors, but it makes a striking, boldly architectural tree. *Yucca elephantipes* 'Variegata' is a variety whose leaves are banded with creamy white along the edges.

RELOCATION: A big specimen is meant to be featured alone and should be dramatized by spotlights. It looks best, I think, in square, shiny white or black modern containers. A single big jade plant (*Crassula argentea*, pages 38–39) in a matching container is a good complement. Or, if you want a group, place aloes (page 27) and agaves (page 25), which are just big rosettes of slim sword-shaped leaves, near it in polished black and white containers on white and black pedestals of different heights. You might prefer coral-red containers and deep electric blue instead of black and white.

SITUATIONS WANTED: Yuccas are desert plants native to Mexico, Central America, and the southern United States. They thrive in temperatures to 70 degrees in the day and as low as 55 degrees at night. Fresh air and strong light are necessities. If you want the plant to grow, give it direct sun in a bright east or west window or a few feet from a south window. A big plant probably can maintain itself under overhead fluorescents augmented by some hours of direct sun daily; you can beef up the footcandles delivered by burning fluorescents at night.

SALARY REQUIREMENTS: Let the soil become quite dry on the surface before you water. Remove whatever water is left in the saucer an hour later. Yucca stands neglect more readily than overwatering. Feed all-purpose plant food alternately with cactus and succulent plant food, switching off every six months. Top dress the plant annually with three parts all-purpose soil and one part sand. Wipe the leaves clean a few times a year if you can.

FYI: Overwatering and shortage of light spoil the plant.

Yucca elephantipes

5
Climbers and Vines

A great big hanging basket of wandering jew costs relatively little; keeping it pruned to keep it beautiful, you'll get tip cuttings enough to supply the entire office with baby plants. And therein lies the good and the bad of climbing and vining plants. The decorating effect is big for a small investment, for these plants are generous, but the maintenance on most is higher than for other kinds of plants.

However, there are jobs that basket plants and vines can do that no other plants do quite as well. The tumbled, jumbled growth of stems and proliferation of leaves bring grace and charm to linear groups of office trees and shrubs, to barren windows, grimy skylights, gawky bookcases, and frigid washrooms. They're great in planters and on top of pedestals in dull corners.

Vining plants have a humorous side, too. I once saw a terribly pompous statue in a decorator's office, one of those marble affairs with a balding head and a bulbous nose, and over it in a mustache effect was creeping a small-leafed English ivy (*Hedera helix*). It gave a whole new dimension to the gentleman sitting behind the desk. He was an imposing man with a very dry way of speaking, but he had chosen the little ivy as a clue to the warmth and humor obscured by the facade.

1 *Ceropegia woodii;* 2 *Passiflora;* 3 *Hedera helix;* 4 *Philodendron oxycardium;* 5 *Tradescantia*

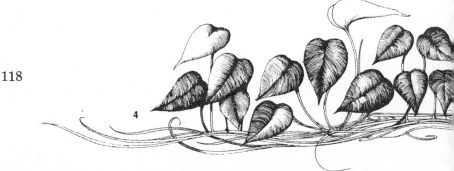

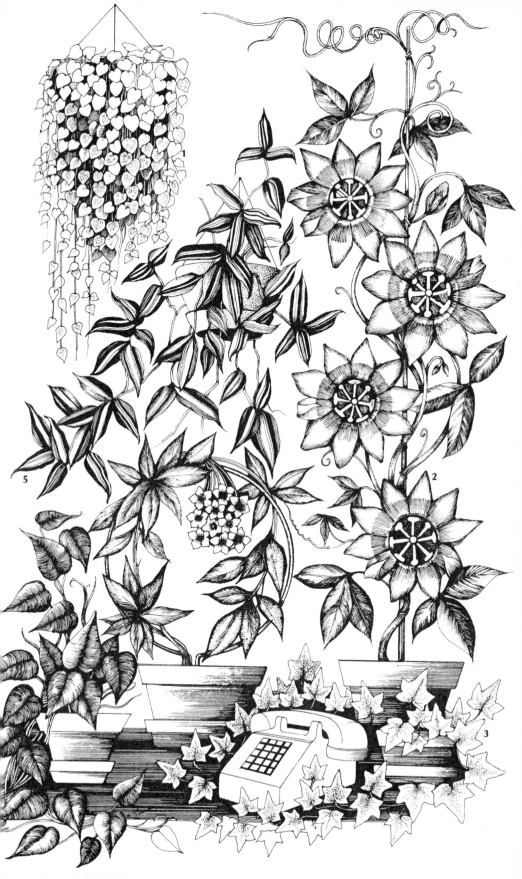

Containers

Containers for plants to be hung in baskets should be unobtrusive. Basket plants generally are sold in white or green plastic pots with attached saucers. Don't buy a basket that doesn't have an attached saucer, or the excess water will drip onto your office floor or desk. Wire mesh baskets lined with moss are pretty but usable only outdoors.

When buying a basket with an attached saucer, make sure the saucer is going to remain attached to the basket. Various makes of saucers are attached in various ways to the pots. Some are permanently fixed to them. These are my preference because once you've lost the saucer (or it has cracked or won't snap back on), it is impossible to replace, which means the whole basket has to be disposed of, since you can't water office plants that are going to drip.

Vining plants don't have to be basket plants unless they are to be hung. They can be planted in any regular pot as long as it is tall enough so that the stems can cascade over the side. For plants whose stems are going to grow very long and hang down several feet, choose plastic containers with rims that curve outward. A soft smooth surface allows tender new stems to grow without damage. You can get a nice effect by placing several potted vining plants in a big square container, wood or wicker, and hanging that.

Hanging the Basket Plants

You can hang basket plants from hooks in the ceiling, from brackets braced against a wall or window jam, from pipes, or brass rods. Before you hang a basket plant, there are a couple of things you must be sure of: Is the hook strong enough to hold the weight of the plant when it is fully mature and has been watered, and will the surface the hook is screwed into take the weight? If you are fixing a hook in a plaster or plasterboard ceiling, best use a molly plug, just as you do when hanging a

1 *Asparagus densiflorus sprengeri;* 2 *Cissus rhombifolia;* 3 *Senecio mikanioides;* 4 *Scindapsus aureus;* 5 *Tradescantia;* A pulley; B weight for pulley; C screwhook and swivel; D wood screws; E ceiling beam; F Lucite bracket

heavy picture or mirror. The same cautions apply to brackets: The bracket itself must be strong enough to handle the plant soaking wet, and the wall into which the bracket is nailed or screwed must be able to handle the stress. I can still remember the big basketful of wandering jew, just watered, whose bracket pulled loose from the wall. It turned upside down as it hit the desk and and then landed facedown on the floor in a shower of plaster. Molly plugs offer security. Follow package instructions for placing them in the wall or ceiling.

Pipes or brass rods, like those used to hang curtains make great supports for basket plants hung in windows, as long as the rods and their brackets are solid enough to take the weight. Recently, I've seen some fascinating trolleys meant to hold several baskets across the span of a big window: The holders to which the basket hooks are to be fixed can be moved to change the location of the baskets. One kind of trolley offered is designed to screw into the bottom of a valance board and seems very well thought out and solid. By hanging baskets at different heights on this sort of trolley, you can create a truly lovely window garden.

If you are planning to hang baskets from the ceiling, the only practical arrangement is to hang them from a pulley that has a weight you can raise, lowering the plant to comfortable watering level. The kind of pulley whose control cord must be tied around something to hold it forces you to place the basket near a wall. A pulley arrangement is the only practical way to hang a plant in a skylight, but to tell the truth, I favor pulleys for all basket plants. I am 5 feet 2½ inches tall, and even in 4-inch heels, I can't water a basket plant hanging in the average window except by standing on a chair—hard in 4-inch heels!

To hang basket plants, use 40-pound test nylon fishing line. Don't use string! Replace wire hangers attached to your basket with this line too; then the plants seem to be suspended in midair. Be sure your bracket or hook is so placed that there's room between the window or wall and the outer edges of the basket. Measure the plant before you buy the bracket to be sure it is wide enough.

When placing a basket plant in an office window or hanging one from a ceiling, make sure it is high up enough to clear the head of the tallest person likely to pass near or under it. Expect to raise that height as the plant's stems grow longer, or else plan to pinch back the stems as they grow too low to be attractive or practical. Stems that reach below the bottom of the container to a distance twice the height of the container look best, as in plants such as German ivy and grape ivy. However, within that context, place the baskets as low as you can because air near the ceiling tends to be hotter and drier—not good for new growth of most plants.

Pruning

When you buy a basket plant, it usually is a big fluffy ball. But with time, the stems lengthen and it can get to be a straggly eyesore. The way to avoid that with most of the vines is to pinch new growth back ruthlessly.

Pinching is illustrated on page 123. New growth is so tender that your fingernails can be the pruning shears! How often should you pinch back? It depends on the plant and on how quickly it is growing. In ideal light, described on the pages that

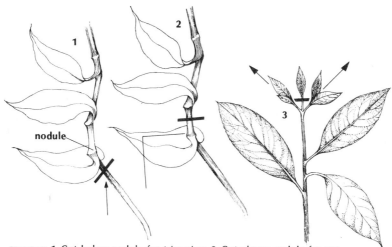

PRUNING: **1** Cut below nodule for trimming. **2** Cut above nodule for propagation. **3** Pinching growth here allows branching.

follow, the vines grow quickly; they're nearly all rapid growers anyway. In less light, they may just maintain themselves and grow hardly at all. I don't think my *Hoya carnosa* has grown 3 inches in three years; it gets hardly any light, has never been fed, and I regularly forget to water it. (Don't follow my example!) If you have a big, beautiful wandering jew you want to keep as is, pinch it every two weeks; if you have a baby English ivy you want to grow big, pinch it once a month or every six weeks. Pinch any time you see a vining plant beginning to look straggly or thin.

If you want to use your trimmings to start new plants, let the stems grow 3 to 6 inches long before you pinch back.

I find it very hard to pinch out or prune back plants. It always feels as though I'm removing a friend's arm, which is why I end up planting cuttings of any and almost every possible size. Terrariums, the base soil of big plants, a small vase with water in it are good places for disposing of tip cuttings, and trying to root them in such spots is one way of postponing the decision whether to discard the cut tips or to acquire lots of new plants.

A good way to turn a small basket plant into a big one is to transplant it to a big basket and to poke all the tip cuttings into the soil around the parent plant.

Watering

At home, the best way to water several basket plants or plants located high up is to put a handful of ice cubes on the soil. It melts slowly and makes no mess though most plants prefer tepid water. This works for plants that like to be cool and require constantly moist soil rather than the occasional drenching.

At work, unless you have a freezer available, the only way to water is with a watering can. It's easiest if you have a foot-stool or if your baskets are on weighted pulleys that let you lower the plant easily (see Hanging the Basket Plants).

If you can, water plants on high shelves and hanging plants in stages: Add a little, then move on to water other plants, and come back to the first plants; if you add a lot of water all at once, it may overflow the drainage saucers. Add a little at a time until you can feel the saucer is beginning to fill with water, then don't add any more.

Feeding

Since these plants tend to grow more rapidly than many other plants, some require more food than I've recommended for plants listed in other chapters. When you read on the following pages, "Feed as package directs," it's not a mistake; I mean it. Only if the plant is not growing at all should you feed it less. When you are encouraging young vines to become big, you may want to feed a little more often than I've suggested, so follow plant food container directions.

Decorating

The twelve vining plants described in this chapter can be used in various ways. If you want big, full baskets to hang in windows or to cascade from file cabinets or pedestals or to place on low stands with groups of shrubs and trees, choose wandering jew (*Tradescantia*), or grape ivy or kangaroo vine (Cissus species); these become played out in a year or two but can be replaced by new baskets of rooted tip cuttings from the parent

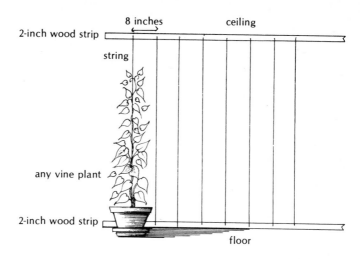

8 inches   ceiling

2-inch wood strip

string

any vine plant

2-inch wood strip

floor

plants. A big mature basket of English ivy (*Hedera helix*) can be used for these purposes, too; English ivy is long-lived once established. Young plants of any of these three can be used to create a lovely green spill over the end of a bookcase, on a washroom countertop, or on a windowsill.

If you want a plant that will grow all around a bare window or twine along the edges of a skylight, then plant passion flower (Passiflora species). It will bloom in good light, giving a show of white, red, or blue from sparse but lovely flowers that last just a day. *Philodendron oxycardium*, sometimes sold as Philodendron cordatum, will climb this way, too, and so will pothos (*Scindapsus aureus*) with a little help.

P. oxycardium also makes a great staking plant. Fill a big tub with lots of young plants, add a totem pole of moss or a bark log as a stake, and you can develop a tall rather imposing show for the reception area. As this plant grows, the leaves get bigger—much bigger—if it is staked and the conditions are right. You can use pothos and nephthytis (*Syngonium podophyllum*) the same way, too. Wax plant (*Hoyo carnosa*), with its waxy, gray-green-pink leaves and extraordinary blooms, can be trained over a wire or up a stake and used for a similar effect; but this one takes time to grow.

Rosary vine (*Ceropegia woodii*) is different; its heart-shaped leaves, twined and tangled on long threads, really show best only hanging in a pretty basket. And creeping fig (*Ficus pumila*), with its tiny leaves, should also have a place all its own where it is shown off to advantage. Both creeping fig and English ivy can be trained to climb a wall by using stringers of clear fishing line nailed to a strip of white wood near the ceiling. Use screw eyes at top and bottom to hold the line. Planters for this purpose should be not less than 8 inches wide by 8 inches deep (12 by 12 inches is better), and plants should be spaced 6 to 8 inches apart. Little aereal roots will help hold the plants to the wall if the wall has a rough surface. You can use the same method to lead ivy or creeping fig up an ugly column, around a boring corner, or over any eyesore, as long as the light is right.

You can start an office collection of vining plants by buying babies. Many are used in big terrariums—wandering jew, nephthytis, pothos, English ivy, grape ivy, for instance. Creeping fig, especially *F. p. minima*, whose leaves are only ½ inch long, can start out carpeting a terrarium or the soil at the foot of a larger plant.

Selection

In addition to the vining plants described in this chapter, there are others located in Chapter 2 among the desk plants and in Chapter 6 among the flowering plants. Those among the desk plants that grow into large basket plants are spider plant (*Chlorophytum comosum*), the ferns, Swedish ivy (*Plectranthus australis*), strawberry begonia (*Saxifraga sarmentosa*), and piggyback plant (*Tolmiea menziesii*).

I've left out of this book altogether some good vining plants that are hard to find in many areas, among them baby smilax (*Asparagus asparagoides myrtifolius*), burrow's tail (*Sedum morganianum*), *Rhipsalis*, and rosary vine (*Clerodendrum thomsonae*). In warm regions, you sometimes can find the staghorn ferns (*Platycerium*) for sale as well as *Stephanotis floribunda*, which is commonly called the Madagascar jasmine; it is a beautiful flowering evergreen that does best with its feet in shade and its head in the sun. *Fatshedera lizei*, which is discussed under *Fatsia japonica* (page 78), is grown indoors as a climber in California, and in my area we treat it as an indoor shrub; staked, it climbs slowly and makes a handsome show. Its common name is climbing aralia.

The Plants

Asparagus densiflorus sprengeri
ASPARAGUS FERN

RESUMÉ: This is a graceful basket or pedestal plant with fluffy, feathery fronds that cascade downward and are covered with soft green needles. Fronds grow to about 6 feet long. It is usually called asparagus fern, or just sprengeri (pronounced *spreng-err-eye*, with the accent on the *eye*). When conditions are right, it produces tiny white flowers that develop into long-lasting bright red berries. It is easy to handle and one of the most beautiful of the indoor plants.

RELOCATION: Sprengeri in small sizes is a lovely plant for the corner of a sunny desk or in a window. Raised on an upturned flowerpot, it can do wonders for a barren file cabinet. Two or three hanging from different length nylon filaments or fishing lines brighten boring corners and dull walls in just about any area.

SITUATIONS WANTED: Sprengeri are grown in bright light in humid greenhouses. Newly purchased plants placed in less light than provided by the grower or near the ceiling where the air is hot, stale, and dry will turn yellow and drop needles. Ideal light is indirect sun from an east or west window or a bright north window. In summer, move your plant back a few feet out of hot direct sunlight. Young plants grow well under fluorescent lights and may succeed under strong desk lamplight. The plants need fresh air.

SALARY REQUIREMENTS: Keep the soil evenly moist or you'll lose foliage. If this happens, cut the bare branches back to where foliage grows. Since the soil is usually very porous, water goes right through and is dripping on the floor before you know it, so try a daily cupful for a big basket. That should maintain even moisture. Mist daily, especially if temperatures are in the 70s. Feed all-purpose plant food half as often as directed on the package. Repot annually in all-purpose soil. Sprengeri is more likely to flower and produce berries if set out in summer in light similar to the light it grows in indoors, choose an airy cool location.

FYI: Red spider mites are a problem in hot stale air. Air often and increase frequency of misting.

Ceropegia woodii
ROSARY VINE

RESUMÉ: This is the basket plant to choose when you want something small and different (except in California, where it can be hard to find). In a year it will dangle (and tangle) stringy, wiry stems to 5 feet long down the pot sides on which tiny heart-shaped pairs of leaves grow at wide interstices. They're blue with an overlay of silver. The stems show here and there little round bulbils, like green rosary beads; and in good light a scattering of 1-inch purplish flowers will bloom. It's a fascinating but forgiving little tropical vine that does well in most offices. The plant is also commonly called string-of-hearts and hearts entangled.

RELOCATION: The stems of this vine must dangle freely to look beautiful, so grow rosary vine in a hanging basket. Mature plants need big pots—8 inches across the top—but the foliage will not really envelop the pot, so give the container some thought. White shows off the vines; blue or green blends with the leaf colors and obscures the plant. I saw a small plant in a glazed pottery hanging container of bright red and it looked terrific. Rosary vine also is pretty in a hammered copper basket.

SITUATIONS WANTED: The temperatures that suit you best suit rosary vine, but the plant needs some sun to bloom and look its best. An east, west, or bright north window are suitable, or near a south window that gets the sun at a slant for a few hours a day. Don't hang rosary vine above a radiator.

SALARY REQUIREMENTS: Allow the soil to dry a little before you water but not completely. Then really drench the plant, and let excess remain in the saucer for an hour before removing. If the plant reabsorbs all the water, add more to see how much it will take. Measure the amount of water used for future reference. Feed all-purpose plant food at half strength as often as package directs. If it outgrows its original container, repot in three parts all-purpose soil and one part sand. Cut back when the stems get ugly. Bulbils on stems will root in moist vermiculite and give you baby plants to pot.

FYI: Mealybugs love rosary vine.

Cissus Species
KANGAROO VINE
GRAPE IVY

RESUMÉ: These are medium-size luxurious climbers from the tropics, and among them are one or two of the best basket plants for low light—*Cissus antarctica,* the kangaroo vine, and *C. rhombifolia,* grape ivy. The kangaroo vine has 4-inch leaves that are shiny, pointed, and deeply quilted. Grape ivy is more decorative, I think; it has three leaflets which are reddish underneath to each brown stem and tendrils. It produces tiny white flowers and grows so rapidly it makes a full plant even in poor light. Kangaroo vine grows vigorously, too. Either can be trained to grow up or down. There's another kind, *C. discolor,* with red stems and velvety leaves that are reddish-purple underneath, that grows better in warm humid locations.

RELOCATION: A corner shelf in a washroom is a good spot for cissus; so is the edge of a big bookcase or the top of a file cabinet (as long as the plant can creep down over the edge) or a tall plant stand in a boring corner (turn a 75- or 100-watt spotlight on it).

SITUATIONS WANTED: Cissus can stand a lot of mistreatment, but it grows fastest if there is warmth—75-degree days, nights to 65 degrees—and fresh air and humidity. In dim light cissus will maintain itself. It will grow luxuriantly in bright light from an east or west window; two or three hours of direct sunlight a day are ample. And it does well under overhead fluorescents. If the light is too low, the plants soon complain via new growth that is small and spindly.

SALARY REQUIREMENTS: Keep the soil a little moist. It should be not quite dry on the surface before you water. Drench the plant until excess appears in the saucer; an hour later, empty the saucer. Mist as often as you can. Prune to suit the location. Three- or 4-inch tip cuttings root easily in moist soil or vermiculite. Feed all-purpose plant food year round at half the rate recommended; don't miss if the plant is growing a lot. Repot as needed in all-purpose potting soil. Shower monthly to keep the shiny leaves clean.

FYI: Drafts of hot dry air cause leaves to drop.

Ficus pumila
CREEPING FIG

RESUMÉ: Years ago I fell in love with a weeping fig (*Ficus benjamina*) in a west-window garden, and I've been in love with all the small-leaved figs ever since. The adorable little plant called creeping fig just turns my knees to jelly. Marlon Brando never affected me more! Creeping fig has tiny inch-long heart-shaped, bright green leaves and will creep or climb or spill down the sides of a dish. There's a variety called *F. pumila minima* with leaves only ½ inch long. It grows very slowly. And there's a gorgeous variegated creeping fig with leaves edged in white or cream.

RELOCATION: One of the most striking uses of creeping fig is training it to grow up a semisunny wall of rough brick, like a blanket of ivy. Tip cuttings of this plant will root, so you could start a few creeping figs on the wall side of a narrow planter 18 inches deep and front them with coleus (page 37) on the people side to keep the view pretty while the fig grows up the wall. One of the prettiest dish gardens is a terracotta bowl on a pedestal, planted with *Ficus pumila*, both plain and variegated, a just-rooted *Dizygotheca elegantissima* (page 75), a showy coleus (page 37), and a young rex begonia (page 32). Or root tip cuttings at the foot of a ficus or kentia palm (*Howeia fosteriana*, page 108).

SITUATIONS WANTED: Lots of air, but no cold drafts, with an hour or two of full sun in a bright window suit this and most any other ficus, as long as the rest of the day it has bright light. Because this fig is little and needs fewer footcandles of light than a big fig, small plants should adapt to desk light with additional light from overhead fluorescents.

SALARY REQUIREMENTS: Keep the soil evenly moist. Empty the saucer an hour after watering. Mist daily when temperatures are over 72 degrees; air often by opening windows or turning on an air conditioner, especially if the planting is big. Feed all-purpose plant food. Repot as needed in all-purpose soil over 1 inch of pebbles for drainage. Shower small plants monthly.

FYI: Dried-out or soggy soil can kill a small plant very quickly. Dry air invites red spider, so mist often.

Hedera helix
ENGLISH IVY

RESUMÉ: English ivy comes in small-leaved forms, fuzzy little plants that are for my taste among the brightest, greenest, and prettiest of the indoor vining and basket plants. Once acclimatized, they're durable and will go on forever if repotted now and then, and they'll serve any purpose you choose from carpeting a terrarium floor to feathering a topiary. 'Glacier' is quite small leaved and is several shades of gray green, margined white, and edged in an unlikely pink. 'Edward Jr.,' a variety similar to 'Glacier,' has no pink. 'Conglomerata Minima' and 'Needlepoint' are very slow growing. 'Needlepoint's' leaves are only ½ inch long. 'Shamrock' has red stems and tiny leaves. You'll easily find all these and dozens more at almost any greenhouse.

RELOCATION: Varieties that grow energetically, 'Glacier' or 'Merion Beauty,' make glorious hanging baskets and planter edgers. Carpet the office terrarium or a tiny desk terrarium with 'Needlepoint,' or set a planter full of fast-growing ivy by an old brick wall, and train the ivy on fishing line to climb the wall.

SITUATIONS WANTED: Ivy takes time, sometimes months, to begin growing, but once acclimatized, it is long-lived and durable. Temperatures between 60 and 70 degrees are best, and it can go down to 50 degrees at night. Ivy needs fresh air; it grows rapidly in either full sun or several hours of direct sun daily. It will adapt to less light, even that of a bright desk lamp.

SALARY REQUIREMENTS: Water ivy enough to keep it evenly moist, not soggy. If light is low, don't overwater and be sure to empty the saucer one hour after watering. Mist daily if heat is over 70 degrees. Repot in all-purpose soil as roots crowd the container or every four or five months for slow growers. Feed all-purpose plant food every two weeks if plants are growing fast and hardly ever if plants aren't growing. Root 6-inch cuttings in moist vermiculite to start new plants. Pinch out tips of growing plants monthly to keep them dense. Shower plants monthly if you can.

FYI: Red spider mites are a hazard in hot dry air.

Hoya carnosa
WAX PLANT

RESUMÉ: Hoya leaves are waxy looking, but it is the flower that gives this plant its common name; it is a fragrant cluster of starry little blooms centered around a bright red or purple eye, and it truly looks as though it is made of wax. Hoya grows slowly indoors and is sparsely leaved compared, for instance, with Swedish ivy. The stem is thick and stiff and easily trained to various shapes, as around a circular wire support (florists sell them). *Hoya carnosa* has green leaves; *H. c. variegata* has bluish leaves edged in cream white with a tinge of pink; and *H. bella* is a dwarf with deep green leaves and waxy white flowers with purple centers.

RELOCATION: Hoya is often put in poor light, where it grows little, collects dust, and is a bore. Give it a beautiful glazed ceramic pot in a brilliant blue or cranberry red, or put it in a polished aluminum cube and place it at eye level on a reception room end table, and it is a beauty. Once full grown, it makes a splendid hanging basket.

SITUATIONS WANTED: To turn hoya into a beautiful plant, provide a moderately warm climate, 70–75 degrees; fresh air; and good light, either several hours of full sun or some sun and fluorescent lights overhead. A spotlight (not too close or it burns the leaves) will dramatize the plant and provide extra foot-candles of light.

SALARY REQUIREMENTS: Let the soil dry out a little on the surface before you water (hoya can take drought but won't grow in it) ; drench until excess fills the saucer, and empty the saucer an hour later. Mist often in temperatures over 75 degrees, and shower or sponge the leaves monthly. If the plant can summer outdoors, blooming is a probability. Feed all-purpose plant food to encourage foliage on a small plant; feed blooming-type plant food to encourage flowers after the plant has grown some. Blooms appear on spurs that grow on the branches. Do not remove the spurs when you remove dead blooms; more flowers will grow on the spurs. Repot as needed in all-purpose soil.

FYI: Cold temperatures combined with soggy soil are bad news for the wax plant.

Passiflora Species
PASSION FLOWER

RESUMÉ: In the tropics, this is a really fast-growing vine with big showy flowers in a variety of colors, great to train around the upper reaches of an office. The leaves are simple and on the small side and grow rather sparsely, particularly indoors. The flowers appear all year long and last a day. The word *passion* here refers to the Crucifixion and was inspired by the unusual shape of the flowers. In New York it is easier to find white or blue passion flowers than other colors, which may be pink or purple. In California indoor plants are rare. These plants, like many other rapid growers, may begin to look seedy at the end of a year, but they can easily be replaced by starting tip cuttings.

RELOCATION: If you have a bleak window with a bleak view or a big skylight that needs help, put a potful of passion flower vines to work. With transparent fishing line to guide the tendrils, the plants will climb up or around or sideways. Several plants in a pot or a hanging basket, with the vines from all the plants following the same lead lines, will fill your panes with greenery and a sprinkling of flowers all year long.

SITUATIONS WANTED: Good light is essential for bloom. The sunlight need not be direct, but there must be bright light reaching the window most of the day. *Passiflora* is a tropical vine, and it can take quite a lot of heat—the kind you get up near the ceiling—as long as there is lots of humidity in the air. Airing the room now and then helps keep the plant vigorous and beautiful.

SALARY REQUIREMENTS: You can keep a pot of passion flower looking lush by taking frequent tip cuttings (6 inches long) from the end of the growing vines and rooting them right in the original pot. Always keep the soil evenly moist but never soggy. An hour after watering, empty the saucer so the plant doesn't sit in water. Feed blooming-type plant food as directed on the package. Yearly, in early spring, start a new pot from tip cuttings in all-purpose soil.

FYI: High and dry heats or soggy soil can spoil the plant.

Philodendron oxycardium

RESUMÉ: Philodendrons are truly indestructible vines, and there's a good reason for their durability: They come from jungles where drenching showers and droughts, cool and heat, humidity and dry air are all common. *Philodendron oxycardium* is a philodendron that has heart-shaped leaves that are small when the plant is young. It is a climber; properly cared for and staked on a bark log, the leaves grow to 12 inches in size. In California, *P. rubrum* is more common in offices; its leaves are a deep reddish green. *P. oxycardium* is sometimes known as P. cordatum.

RELOCATION: You can start this plant as a hanging basket plant; I have a pair meant to droop, but the lead vines are inching at right angles across my wall toward the window. They would enjoy more light, they are saying, and don't like hanging. Philodendron can be trained to climb around a bookcase or up and around office trees. Four-inch tip cuttings root easily in vermiculite and make neat little desk plant gifts for coworkers.

SITUATIONS WANTED: Philodendrons do well in average office temperatures, down to 60 degrees or so, and in semisunny or semishady light. But if you supply warmth and high humidity, you'll find this a lush full vine that grows vigorously. Light to the side of an east or west window, in a north window, or several feet back from a south window are all okay. Fluorescents and desk lamps are fine sources of light, too.

SALARY REQUIREMENTS: Keep the soil evenly moist to keep this plant at its best. However, it can stand neglect; a few leaves may yellow, but even if the whole vine begins to wither, watering generally will bring it back. Don't let it stand in puddles, however; empty the saucer an hour after watering. Mist as often as you can to promote good growth. Feed all-purpose plant food as directed on the package. Repot in all-purpose soil when roots jam the pot. Sponge leaves clean monthly if you can. If you stake the plant, as suggested above, and can keep the stake moist, philodendron will grow fuller and more beautiful all the time.

FYI: Cold dry air and soggy soil are enemies of philodendron.

Scindapsus aureus
POTHOS
DEVIL'S IVY

RESUMÉ: Pothos is a beautiful plant that is a little like *Philodendron oxycardium* and just about as durable. A tropical climber, it has long heart-shaped leaves that are a brilliant green splashed with yellow; the leaves are crisper than philodendron leaves and so shiny they looked waxed. It's a relative of *Monstera*, and when staked and growing in perfect conditions, it will eventually develop leaves to 2 feet across, deeply cut like *Monstera*. The prettiest pothos are types variegated in white; the kind called 'Marble Queen' sometimes seems to be white spotted with green rather than the other way around. It is lovely but withstands overwatering less than the other kinds. 'Tricolor' is splashed with pale green and cream; there is also a variety tinged with apricot.

RELOCATION: Pothos is really handsome when there are several plants growing in a big copper, brass, or wood bucket. Train some strands to a bark log, a moss stake, or a trellis, and let others spill over the sides and down. Pothos is nice, too, in big hanging baskets or trained to grow up the side of a bright window on transparent fishing line. Tip cuttings are lovely in dish gardens (only for a brief time, since they tend to outgrow these) or on top of a reception area table or desk.

SITUATIONS WANTED: Warm temperatures and bright light coupled with humidity make pothos grow like crazy and keep the variegations beautiful. Temperatures to 80 degrees, but not below 60 degrees, are fine. Ideal light is to the side of an east or west window, beside a south window, or in a north window. Under fluorescents, recessed ceiling spots, and desk lamps plants do remarkably well, though variegations may fade.

SALARY REQUIREMENTS: Let the soil dry a little between waterings. Empty the saucer one hour after watering. Mist often in high heats and shower or sponge the leaves monthly. Feed all-purpose plant food half as often as package directs. Repot in African violet soil when roots crowd pots; add 2 inches of gravel for drainage. Tip cuttings of any length will root and even grow in vermiculite or water.

FYI: Soggy soil is the enemy of pothos.

Senecio mikanioides
GERMAN IVY

RESUMÉ: German ivy looks a lot like the large-leaved ivies, and though it can take a little more heat than *Hedera helix*, it flourished in the cool parlors of Victorian homes. When conditions are right, it produces clusters of daisylike blooms, yellow and faintly fragrant. There are variegated types whose leaves are yellow and green. The plant is from South Africa and is a very tolerant office plant that grows fairly rapidly. It's hard to find in California, so plan to use *Hedera helix* if you live in that state.

RELOCATION: Several German ivies in a big basket make a beautiful hanging plant for a bright window; small plants grown from tip cuttings are handsome desk plants. A full German ivy is a lovely plant to let tumble over the side of a gawky bookcase or a graceless office file cabinet, especially if you pinch it often enough to keep it full. It thrives in a washroom window or under fluorescents on a pedestal in a washroom since it loves moisture.

SITUATIONS WANTED: Good light, a moderately cool room, and fresh air are keys to success with German ivy. A bright east or west window, but without direct sun, is ideal. Some window light coupled with fluorescents is okay, too, or place your ivy in a bright north window. High temperatures can be between 70 and 75 degrees (while the English ivies do best between 65 and 70 degrees) as long as there is lots of fresh air and moisture. Nighttime lows can be to 55 degrees. Avoid hot drafts; don't place this plant near forced-air heat.

SALARY REQUIREMENTS: Keep the soil evenly moist. Empty the saucer an hour after watering. Mist the plant often and air the room by opening windows or turning on the air conditioner, especially if heat is over 70 degrees. Feed all-purpose plant food half as often as package directs. When roots become crowded, repot in all-purpose soil over 2 inches of gravel for drainage. Keep tips pinched out so the plant will grow bushy. Shower occasionally if you can; a splash or two of ordinary tap water will do the trick.

FYI: Drafts of hot, dry air wither new growth, especially when there is no moisture in the air.

Syngonium podophyllum
NEPHTHYTIS
ARROWHEAD PLANT

RESUMÉ: This is a rapid-growing climber with leaves shaped like very large arrowheads, and it makes a wonderful display when staked and trained to a big bark half log or a moss tree or totem pole. There are many varieties with fascinating and beautiful markings. The kind incorrectly called Nephthytis triphylla has silver-white centers and veins when young, but the markings fade as the leaves mature; 'Dot Mae' is similar but the variegations last longer; 'Tricolor' is pale green with cream variegations; the leaves of 'Imperial White' are greenish white with a narrow green border.

RELOCATION: Young plants make attractive desk plants and beautiful hanging baskets. The leaves of the variegated sorts are most strongly marked at this stage. When a plant begins to grow lengthy, move it to a bookcase or a divider partition and allow it to cascade. To develop a big, beautiful tall plant, pot four plants in a 13-inch tub with a large half log or moss totem at the back; stake two plants and let the others fall over the side.

SITUATIONS WANTED: Nephthytis prefers filtered light and no direct sun; it can be to the side of an east or west window or in a bright north window, or give some light from any of these sources coupled with overhead fluorescents. Young plants do well just with overhead fluorescents or a desk lamp. Warm temperatures—75 to 80 degrees during the days—are welcome as long as there is moisture in the air. Low temperatures can be to 65 degrees at night.

SALARY REQUIREMENTS: Keep the soil evenly moist. The plant stands some drying out and is very forgiving, but it won't thrive without some moisture. Empty the saucer an hour after watering. Mist often in temperatures over 75 degrees in winter. Feed all-purpose plant food half as often as package directs. When roots crowd containers, repot in all-purpose soil over 2 inches of pebbles for drainage. Six-inch tip cuttings root easily in soil or moist vermiculite. Pruning tips doesn't make it bush out, so pinch back only if it grows out of bounds.

FYI: Red spider mites and mealybugs occasionally attack.

Tradescantia Species
WANDERING JEW

RESUMÉ: Wandering jew is such an easy, fast-growing plant that it generally gets mistreated; stuck in a dim light the leaves grow sparse on skinny stems, and no one sees its beautiful markings. The leaves aren't showy, though some are backed with purple and have purple stems, but many kinds have an iridescence that is breathtaking if you take the time to look. The plants grow very quickly into big leafy baskets, so large plants aren't costly compared to other plants in similar sizes. (Buy a middle-size basket; the big ones tend to play out soon.) *Tradescantia fluminensis variegata* is one of the plants officially listed as wandering jew; however, there are others given that common name. If you want a wandering jew with a purple-silver and green leaf, ask for *Zebrina pendula*; *T. f. variegata* has a green leaf striped white.

RELOCATION: When you're thinking of a hanging basket for the office, you are probably seeing a wandering jew in your imagination. It's a great plant for any bright window or an interior spot where an ebullient small-leaved plant would brighten things. It can hang over bookcase corners, dangle from file cabinets, or drip from washroom shelves as long as ledge edges don't cut the succulent, rather delicate stems.

SITUATIONS WANTED: Ideal conditions are provided by a bright light in an east, west, or a few feet from a south window and a rather cool interior—70 degrees, down to 55 degrees at night. It will grow spindly in less light and higher heats. Air often by opening windows or turning on an air conditioner.

SALARY REQUIREMENTS: Let the soil dry slightly before watering, then drench the plant until lots of water fills the saucer. An hour later, empty the saucer. Mist often if heat is over 70 degrees. Feed all-purpose plant food as package directs. Pinch tips very often to keep the plant bushy and beautiful. Tip cuttings, 10 inches long, placed in a vase of water in a big bunch make an instant plant, and they'll grow there happily enough for months. When your original plant begins to show browned leaves, start lots of cuttings in water or moist vermiculite; when rooted, pot them in all-purpose soil.

FYI: Hot stale air encourages red spider mites.

6
Color and Bloom

The flowering plants that will bloom well in your office aren't many, but it really is so exciting to see the little buds form and begin to open their brilliant drops of color that I find them irresistible. Some, like the cheery little African violets (*Saintpaulia*) with their pink and purple blossoms, bloom all year round, so you soon become accustomed (if not exactly jaded!) to their flowering. But when your first orchid begins its one, two, or three cycles of bloom—flowers that last four to six weeks —it is a thrilling experience.

African violets and the wax begonias (*Begonia semperflorens*) and impatiens (*Impatiens walleriana sultani*) are reliable all-year bloomers. They're small plants, desk size, and once they begin to flower, they usually go right on doing so. The low-growing African violets grouped under fluorescent lights in a bookcase or wall garden make a showy display, and when you have VIPS coming, you can take individual pots away from their light source and spot them for a day or two or three without interfering with the blooming.

Browallia in small sizes blooms reliably indoors and is a sweet little plant for your desk, but the bloom is less lavish with these than with the ones previously mentioned. *Oxalis* is another

1 *Thunbergia alata*; 2 *Pelargonium hortorum*; 3 *Saintpaulia*; 4 *Impatiens walleriana sultani*; 5 *Bougainvillea*; 6 *Amaryllis*; 7 *Kalanchoe blossfeldiana*; 8 *Oxalis*; 9 *Cyclamen*

that blooms nearly all the time, but the blooms aren't very showy. These flowering plants are for private enjoyment rather than for office color.

Among the plants that bloom only for a period of time, the most glamorous are the orchids. Those species I've suggested, *Paphiopedilum* and *Phalaenopsis,* are good for beginners and like the other orchids, bloom for a few weeks at one or more intervals during the year. When they bloom depends on the individual variety. These and the miniature roses, *Rosa chinensis minima,* I recommend highly if you have a boring repetitious job, not because they take all that much care, but because they lend so much excitement to your daily routine. The tiny roses bloom heavily for rather long periods in late spring, summer, and early fall, then fall off a little. But these mini replicas of big rose bushes are adorable just as foliage plants.

Easter cactus (*Rhipsalidopsis gaertneri*), is another exotic seasonal bloomer—a big one produces a spectacular shower of flowers. Its odd, cascading, clawlike jointed stems are fascinating year round.

A seasonal bloomer that is somewhat less spectacular is *Kalanchoe blossfeldiana,* which blooms at Christmas; it's a small shrubby succulent and quite sweet as a desk plant, even out of bloom. There's a whole group of cacti that will flower, but conditions that bring them into bloom aren't always available, so these are grouped under desk plants in Chapter 2. Kalanchoe could join the cacti mentioned there in a little desert garden; in bloom, it would attract a lot of admiration. There's something so touching about those prickly cacti producing bright-colored flowers!

Kalanchoe in a gift wrapping makes a great little Christmas plant, and the bulbs of amaryllis (*Hippeastrum*) make great holiday gifts for coworkers.

Now, if you're looking for something big and splashy that flowers, consider the three vining plants in this chapter. The lipstick vine (*Aeschynanthus speciosus*) is treated as a basket plant, and though it needs TLC to bloom, it's worth the effort because it really puts on a show once it gets going! It blooms in lipstick-shaped flowers—what could be showier than that? A mature *Bougainvillea* trained to a trellis and in full bloom in an office is just a knockout. The blooms actually are bracts (papery leaflike enclosures for the real flowers, which are insignificant) in hot pinks, oranges, and purples. The black-eyed-Susan vine, *Thunbergia alata*, is less showy; it's a climbing plant thick with leaves and usually grown against a trellis, but it draws every eye nevertheless.

I've saved geraniums (*Pelargonium hortorum*) to mention last because I love them best. In a sunny window, they will bloom all year round, producing big fat clusters of blossoms so cheery it only takes one to make you think the whole office is in bloom. And they take heat and neglect without dying. (They grow leggy in poor light, but they grow, nonetheless!)

In addition to the flowering plants named here, there are many plants in other chapters that will flower. Their flowering isn't as reliable, so, to avoid the feeling of failure you get when a plant isn't doing something you are waiting for it to do, I have treated those all as foliage plants. Then, if they bloom, you've got a bonus!

Color in the Office

There are other ways to bring color and bloom to the office besides growing it yourself.

If your office has a budget for plants, arrange with a florist for seasonal bloomers to parcel out among reception tables and office gardens.

Poinsettias in red, pink, white, and marbled appear on the market in masses around Christmas, and in good conditions, they last as long as six months. They do drop a lot of leaves when they first get to work, but generally they recover.

Cyclamen in pink, rose, red, or white lasts a long time when the soil is kept evenly moist. Cyclamen does beautifully in a sunny east or west window or under fluorescent light. Calceolaria, which has brilliant-colored blooms that look like little pocketbooks, responds to the same conditions as cyclamen, and like cyclamen, it likes it a cool atmosphere—60 to 70 degrees.

Potted chrysanthemums are beginning to be offered all seasons of the year, because growers have found they can bring them into bloom by creating long nights and duplicating fall's early darkness, which is their natural blooming season. These are quite inexpensive and last forever if you keep the soil moist.

Hydrangeas, kept moist, will bring blue to your office garden; they're almost the only flowering plant that can. Camelias, if your rooms are cool, will last well, and so will azaleas, which bloom in shrubby clouds of pink, red, or white in early to mid-spring.

And then there are the potted spring bulbs: gloriously scented hyacinths and paper-white narcissus. They will bloom for weeks. There are also tulips and daffodils at that time of year, and for small displays, there are adorable little bluebells and grape hyacinth. (Keep those on the dry side to prolong blooming.)

If your office has no budget for buying live plants, how about dried flowers combined with the growing greens? You can mix little bouquets of dried blue or red salvia, cockscomb, goldenrod, and those bright little puffs called strawflower in among foliage plants to bring a little color relief to the scene. Salvia, lavender with its sweet scent, and celosia all have long slender branches for tall arrangements. Some of the prettiest dried arrangements I've seen were made from wildlings—silvery beach grasses, pussy willow cut in spring before it opened, and Queen Anne's lace. Hung upside down in a warm airy attic or garage, these three dry beautifully and last forever.

In spring and summer, bringing color to the office garden is easy if you live in the country or have connections: friends who garden, or live in the country. If you look closely, you'll find that woods and fields are full of sometimes showy but more often subtle wild flowers; Queen Anne's lace just covers the Northeast in late summer and in fall, and brooms and heathers and cattails abound by the shores of streams. If you pick these wildlings (and garden flowers, too) with your right hand, while holding a pitcher of water ready to receive them in your left, you'll find that they wilt hardly at all. Pick them in the cool of evening or before the sun dries the air in the morning; then they'll last longer. Don't bunch them in your grubby little hot hand while you climb the next hill or they won't last until you get home.

Placement

There are some suggestions in the following pages for placing flowering plants. However, bringing flowering plants into bloom, with a few exceptions, is a matter of catering to the plant's light need first. While the foliage plants will maintain themselves happily in much less light than you might expect or experts recommend, flowering plants generally (*Spathiphyllum clevelandii* is an exception) require some direct sunlight to bloom really well. In California many of the flowering plants in this chapter aren't offered to indoor office gardeners because there the whole emphasis is on keeping the sun out; without sun, many of the plants described in this chapter will not bloom. Since the plant's bloom depends on the light it gets, that means that the flowering plants dictate their own locations and won't gracefully take orders from you.

The way I handle the flowering plants is to select kinds that will bloom in the window light I have (because there the foot-candles are greater), and once they are blooming, I bring them into the interior of the office to brighten various desks, tables, and gardens. Most of them will take one, two, or three days away from their blooming site without dropping a stitch. And orchids, bless their hearts, will stay in bloom even when you move them for several weeks away from their blooming situation.

You can, of course, have whole flowering gardens in bloom if you have low fluorescents in a bookcase or over a wall garden, as described in Chapter 7. You can also keep some bloomers that need strong light flowering under individual spotlights or grow lights. And that's the way to handle matters when you want to keep a flowering plant or several in bloom—right in the middle of a floor garden. If the spotlight spoils the look of the garden, just bring it out in the evenings before you go home and remove it in the morning. (Then everyone will wonder how you got the flowering plant to bloom!) Overhead spots and floods can be handled the same way. Recessed into the ceiling, they can be pointed to hit specific plants that need lots of sun and turned on by automatic timers when the staff leaves at the end of the day.

Watering

Flowering plants need plenty of water as they begin to form buds. Once the blooming begins, the buds will last longer if they are watered a little less than usual. This is particularly true of the bulbs; for instance, hyacinths and tulips (which, by the way, don't need window light once they are in bloom). This is not true of some moisture-loving plants, such as browallia. So take this general suggestion with a grain of salt and study the special requirements of each plant before you apply the rule.

Don't water or mist buds or blooms. That's another general rule. Blooms can be exquisite with a few drops of dewlike water from the watering can, but waterlogged blooms often brown, so be wary of artistic effects. Ice-cold water is bad for most plants; they should be watered with tepid water. However, ice water affects some really badly when it lands on the leaves. African violet leaves show ugly yellow marks when they've been doused with cold water. As a rule, then, it is smart to water flowering plants from beneath the foliage, using *tepid* water.

Feeding

Some more generalizations. Plants that you hope will bloom generally should be especially well fed with a blooming type of plant food in the months before bloom is expected and while blooming is taking place. African violets, on the other hand, bloom all year round, and I feed them all year round but using only about half as much plant food as container directions suggest. Salts in the fertilizers build up in the soil, and unless you are planning to repot the plant often or else can flush the salts out (see directions for flushing roses under *Rosa chinensis minima*, page 161), in time the buildup will affect the plant, and it won't be any good.

Repotting

On the whole, it's a poor idea to repot plants when they are in bloom. When repotted, plants put a lot of effort into growing new roots and seem to forget for a time that their job is to bloom. African violets and wax begonias, which bloom just about all the time, may have to be repotted when in full bloom, so go ahead. Flowering may slow or stop for a bit, but it will resume.

Starting New Plants

I'm sure you know it, but I'll say it anyway: When you start new plants, either by potting root divisions of mature plants or by planting tip cuttings, the new plants will take time to root and establish themselves. Until those basic tasks are accomplished, they won't put their minds to blooming. Baby plants, with few exceptions, take time to come into bloom. This can be significant when you are buying flowering plants. Dealers generally will tell you how long it takes a plant to come into bloom, and of course, some plants will bloom when really very small. But if you want an instant show of color, the only way I know to guarantee it is to buy a plant already blooming.

Containers

On the whole, containers for plants that bloom all year are best when they are unobtrusive. Dark green plastic is the most subtle container available—after that, white plastic pots, and after that, terracotta. Small woven baskets are low-key cachepots for flowering plants, but I sometimes feel flowering plants, like ladies going out to a formal luncheon, need something more finished; however, it had better be a single color (with exceptions noted on the following pages) and may prove to show the plant off best if it is in a nicely glazed ceramic.

Faded Blooms

To keep your plants blooming, be conscientious about pinching out fading blooms. Otherwise, the plants will try to develop seeds in the blossoms (which is one purpose of the bloom) and flowering will slow.

The Plants

Aeschynanthus speciosus
LIPSTICK VINE

RESUMÉ: This is a flowering plant that is usually grown in a hanging basket, and it is spectacular when in bloom—a full cascade of dainty waxy leaves on stems 12 to 18 inches long. The flowers are clusters of tubular blooms bright as lipstick. A mature plant is rather expensive but produces a terrific show of color. Given enough light, the plant blooms intermittently throughout the year.

RELOCATION: The cascading stems show off beautifully on a small pedestal or in a hanging basket. I once saw one in full bloom spotlighted on a modernistic lucite pedestal. The column was set in a deep window ledge with a backdrop of ferns (on the shadow side of the window) and other foliage plants. It was gorgeous, and a show easy enough to reproduce.

SITUATIONS WANTED: Lipstick vine will thrive in a bright north window or under strong fluorescent lights near a bright east or west window; but to guarantee luxuriant bloom, grow it where it will receive half a day of direct sun in winter. In summer move it back just to the side of direct sunlight. Warm temperatures— to 75 or 80 degrees—are okay as long as there is lots of moisture and fresh air. It can take temperatures to 65 or 60 degrees at night.

SALARY REQUIREMENTS: Keep the soil evenly moist but be sure to empty excess water from the saucer an hour after watering. Mist the plant as often as you can, and air the room frequently, especially if temperatures are high. Lack of humidity can prevent flowering. Feed blooming-type plant food following container directions; if you have a young plant and want more foliage, change to all-purpose plant food for three or four months. When roots become crowded, repot in African violet or terrarium soil over 2 inches of pebbles for drainage. The plant plays out eventually, so every year or two in early spring root 3-inch tip cuttings to start a new plant. Don't pinch tips, except to take tip cuttings; otherwise, you'll be removing blooms.

FYI: Hot, dry, stale air can wither flower buds. Light and humidity are essential for good bloom.

Begonia semperflorens
WAX BEGONIAS

RESUMÉ: These are desk-size flowering plants, almost trouble free and quite inexpensive in small sizes. You can even start your own from a package of seed. The leaves are round compared to those of the rex begonias and are either fresh bright green or burgundy toned and have a waxy shine. The blooms are small but quite showy and range from whitish pinks to corals and reds. There are fancy-leaved types, such as 'Charm,' whose almost white leaves are furled like a calla lily; and there are double-flowered kinds whose blooms remind me of tiny roses.. Rieger begonias are a different species that look like taller, showier wax begonias, with red, orangy, or pink blooms; they bloom lavishly indoors in good light.

RELOCATION: Several baby wax begonias in contrasting leaf and flower shades make a colorful dish garden for a sunny desk corner or a deep windowsill. The burgundy-leaved wax begonias with their deep rose flowers are especially good amid any fresh-green foliage plants. A big shallow basketful of rieger begonias in bloom makes a handsome display on a low pedestal or in a window.

SITUATIONS WANTED: Temperatures around 70 degrees in the day are fine and can go as low as 55 degrees at night. Light near a sunny east or west window will keep your begonias blooming, especially if there's a lot of fresh air and moisture. A little direct sunlight coupled with light from overhead fluorescents or light from a 75-watt desk lamp will result in fairly good flowering once the plants have acclimatized. If the plants grow leggy and pale, give them more light.

SALARY REQUIREMENTS: Let the surface soil become dry, then drench the plants until excess seeps into the saucer. One hour later, empty the saucer. Mist the plants as often as you can, and keep tips of the fattest stems pinched back. Feed blooming-type plant food as directed. Root tip cuttings every spring in moist vermiculite, and pot the babies in African violet soil over an inch of pebbles for drainage.

FYI: Hot, dry air and dry soil brown leaf edges.

Bougainvillea Species
BOUGAINVILLEA

RESUMÉ: A 2- or 3-foot bougainvillea in bloom is a breath-taking sight in an office, especially if there's lots of sun, glass, and white in the decor. Outdoors, vines grow big and dense enough to cover houses; indoors, it's an airy plant with pointed dark leaves that make a perfect foil for the hot colors of the leaflike bracts around the flowers. Before a shrub-size bougain-villea reaches you, it has been dwarfed by a medium-size pot and carefully pinched back. That makes big plants expensive. Bougainvillea blooms a little all year but most heavily in fall and winter when handled as described below. Colors most avail-able are hot pinks and purples. There are also orange and burgundy varieties, and occasionally I've seen a white one in a florist window. The showier colors are more effective indoors.

RELOCATION: Florists sell plants small enough to display on desk corners. As the plant grows, repot it in a bigger container and start it up a trellis. Mature plants are showiest when stand-ing against a sun-splashed white wall or against a backdrop of shrubs and trees in a sunny floor garden. The bougainvilleas look well with almost any other tropical plants—palms (Chapter 4) and *Philodendron selloum* (page 82), for instance.

SITUATIONS WANTED: For bougainvillea to bloom, it must have full sun in an east or west window or partial sun near a south window in winter. It needs warm temperatures to flower—nights not below 60 degrees, days between 70 and 75 degrees—and moist fresh air. A baby plant under overhead fluorescents with an added spot or grow light shows some bloom.

SALARY REQUIREMENTS: Allow the surface soil to dry out before watering, then drench the plant; an hour later, empty the saucer. Mist and air often. In spring, prune back to 2 or 3 feet; keep all tips pinched out until July. If you can, summer the plant outdoors in full sun. Feed all-purpose plant food spring and summer; feed blooming plant food late summer, fall, and winter.

FYI: Soggy soil and poor light inhibit blooming.

Browallia
BROWALLIA

RÉSUMÉ: These make glorious hanging baskets; you see them often in summer at the seashore covered with tubular blue or white blooms. (Orange browallia [*Streptosolin jamesonii*] is another species whose culture is similar.) I find that indoors big basket plants of browallia dry out unexpectedly and then lots of branches turn brown. However, small desk-size plants are worth taking the trouble to keep moist, for they bloom all the time; the blues are shaded with lavender and especially lovely against the fresh green leaves.

RELOCATION: Desk-size plants aren't showy, making this a lovely tempered little plant to keep near you. It is a trailer, so plan to raise it on a small plastic cube or a lucite pedestal, or place it in an antique silver or pewter inkwell. Just a few branches tumbling over the edge of a bookcase makes a charming display.

SITUATIONS WANTED: I've had the best luck when I've kept browallia in good light but below or to the side of a window with direct sunlight. A combination of overhead fluorescents, desk lamps, and some light from a window should be enough to keep it blooming. It's a tricky plant to grow in a hot office; dry air draws the moisture from the soil, especially in a small pot, and if browallia dries, it wilts quickly and you lose leaves, blooms, and whole branches. Temperatures of 70 degrees are best, with cool nights to 60 or 65 degrees. It thrives on fresh air and doesn't seem to mind cool drafts.

SALARY REQUIREMENTS: You should keep the soil evenly moist but never soggy. Empty the saucer one hour after watering. Grow the plant on a bed of moist pebbles and mist and air daily if you can. If browallia wilts, it often will come back if showered and watered soon enough; cut away branches that have died. Cut 6-inch branch tips after heavy summer blooming, and root in moist vermiculite or all-purpose soil over 1 inch of pebbles for drainage. Feed blooming-type plant food. Pinch tip ends if plant gets leggy to help it branch out.

FYI: Dry air and high heat spoil the plant.

Crossandra infundibuliformis
CROSSANDRA

RESUMÉ: Crossandra is a desk plant 4 to 12 inches tall that covers itself with small tangerine-colored flowers almost all the time but especially in winter and spring. There's a Swedish kind, 'Mona Wallhed,' with salmon-rose blooms. The leaves are very dark green and glossy, so it's a pretty plant even when not in bloom. Crossandra comes from India; it has always been popular in greenhouses and is very successful there. If you can provide the plant with lots of moisture, it will do well in your office, in the reception area, or in a small lobby.

RELOCATION: Choose clean fresh terracotta containers to accentuate the color of the blooms. Even when young and just 4 inches tall, crossandra often will burst into bloom. Plants that are 12 to 14 inches are showy enough in bloom to brighten a big windowsill or table. Several mature plants together in a big pot are lovely with a backdrop of small ferns or other foliage plants that do well in a semisunny location; for instance, a young neanthe bella palm (*Chamaedorea elegans* 'Bella', page 71) or *Fatsia japonica* (page 78).

SITUATIONS WANTED: Crossandra needs good light and plenty of moisture to bloom well. Temperatures should be on the warm side—70 to 80 degrees—and no lower than 65 degrees at night. Fresh air is important to crossandra. Half a day of sun near an east or west window or overhead fluorescents augmented by a few hours of direct sun daily are ideal. It will probably do well under overhead fluorescents augmented by a closeup spotlight, too.

SALARY REQUIREMENTS: Keep the soil evenly moist. Be sure to empty the saucer of excess water an hour after watering. Mist daily and provide fresh air as often as you can. Feed blooming-type plant food as often as directed on the package and shower the leaves monthly. Tip cuttings taken in March usually will root in moist vermiculite. Root cuttings in African violet or terrarium soil over an inch of gravel to ensure good drainage.

FYI: Lack of moist air spoils the plant.

Hippeastrum
AMARYLLIS

RESUMÉ: Amaryllis is that incredibly big trumpet-shaped flower that blooms in threes on top of a very tall, round succulent stalk produced by a giant bulb; the stalks of some kinds are several feet high. The blooms last several weeks if conditions are right and are showstoppers anywhere. I've included this seasonal bloomer here because the bulbs are relatively inexpensive, because they bloom just three or four weeks after potting, and because they make great office gifts around Christmas. Colors range from deep red through tangerine to white, and there are variegated sorts splashed with contrasting colors. Try the American hybrids; they have narrower petals and to my mind are more attractive than the big Dutch plants.

RELOCATION: Half a dozen potted bulbs with red blooms in a floor garden of trees and shrubs make a spectacular holiday display. Single plants are striking enough to display on a big table in a reception area; wrap the pot in big sheets of tissue paper, pointed ends up around the stem. It has a rather naked look otherwise; the strap-shaped leaves generally appear only after the bloom has matured.

SITUATIONS WANTED: Temperatures to 75 degrees during the day and down to 62 degrees at night are fine. Best light is a sunny east or west window. Bulbs brought into bloom in a sunny spot will go on doing their thing even when moved under fluorescents.

SALARY REQUIREMENTS: Pot new bulbs in all-purpose soil over 2 inches of gravel for drainage. Use pots only 2 inches bigger around than the bulbs. Set the bulbs so only the bottom half is covered by soil. Gently firm them into place. Keep the soil evenly moist but not soggy. After blooming, cut the stem off at the soil level and continue to water and feed blooming-type plant food. Keep the plant in a sunny window until August, then store it in a dark closet, dry, for eight weeks. Remove the dead leaves, repot in fresh soil, set in a sunny window, resume watering and feeding, and the bulbs should come into bloom again.

FYI: Mealybugs are a hazard.

Impatiens walleriana sultani
IMPATIENS

RESUMÉ: Mature impatiens in flower is a 12- to 18-inch very broad mound of dainty leaves on succulent stems and just twinkling with star-shaped blooms in brilliant hot shades of pink, coral, or magenta. There are whites, too as well as variegated kinds. Leaves of some kinds are reddish, some are variegated, and others are light or dark green. It's one of the most popular outdoor plants because it blooms happily in dim locations. Dwarf varieties, only 8 to 12 inches tall and 12 inches across, are my choice for indoor growing. You can start your own plants from seed in African violet soil, or buy young plants in spring at garden centers. You may also move your outdoor impatiens into a sunny spot at the office.

RELOCATION: Half a dozen plants in a big hanging basket or grouped in a low, wide, white plastic pot are charming. The location has to be sunny if there are to be lots of blooms, so think of this primarily as a sill plant. It blooms like crazy in a window greenhouse or in a big south-facing bay window.

SITUATIONS WANTED: Though impatiens will maintain itself in bright light, to bloom well in winter it needs full sun in an east or west window, or better yet, in a sunny south window. Direct sun in a south window in summer may be too much, so move the plant back a few feet. Temperatures can be around 70 degrees in the day and down to 55 degrees at night. Fresh air is essential; in a hot dry spot with dead air, impatiens is the world's most likely host for white fly.

SALARY REQUIREMENTS: Keep the soil evenly moist; if it dries, the leaves wilt and the branches will die. An hour after watering empty the saucer so the soil won't be soggy. Mist and air the plant (open the windows or use the air conditioner) as often as you can to keep white fly and red spider at bay. Feed blooming-type plant food. If planting seed, use African violet soil over 2 inches of gravel for drainage. If you move an outdoor plant in, spray it often to discourage white fly and prune the roots and branches back by a third.

FYI: Dry hot stale air invites white fly and red spider mites.

Kalanchoe blossfeldiana
KALANCHOE

RESUMÉ: Kalanchoe is a small shrubby succulent about 12 inches tall with glossy green leaves edged in red; it blooms around Christmas with showy clusters of tiny flowers in red, orange, or yellow. In the right conditions, it goes on blooming through winter. Dwarf varieties are the bronze-foliaged 'Tom Thumb,' which blooms in red or yellow, and 'Vivid,' which has fresh green leaves and orange-red blooms.

RELOCATION: *Kalanchoe blossfeldiana* in bloom, with a red bow in among the branches and pretty Christmas wrapping paper, makes a charming desk decoration during the holidays. With just overhead fluorescents and a desk lamp to provide light for it, kalanchoe will go on blooming two weeks or more; after the New Year, move it to a sun-splashed window and blooming should pick up again. Even out of bloom, the crisp fresh leaves make this a pleasant foliage plant for the windowsill or a sunny desk or bookcase corner.

SITUATIONS WANTED: To bloom, *K. blossfeldiana* must have bright sun and long nights without any artificial light. Half a day of sun in an east or west window or near a south window should be fine; but make sure not even a streetlight provides footcandles at night. This is not a good choice for buildings where lights are burned 24 hours a day because the plants only come into bloom when nights (real or artificial) grow longer. Ideal temperatures are around 70 degrees in the day and down to 55 degrees at night.

SALARY REQUIREMENTS: If you can keep the plant in darkness from sunset to morning from October 1 until bloom begins, the plant will flower. Plants get played out, so at the end of the blooming season, start new plants from leaf cuttings, using the same method as for African violets. Put in half-and-half all-purpose soil and cactus mix; feed all-purpose plant food to new plants from spring until mid-September, then switch to blooming-type plant food. Water only when surface soil begins to feel dry; then drench the plant and empty the saucer of the excess water one hour later.

FYI: Light shortage spoils foliage and inhibits bloom.

Oxalis Species
FOUR-LEAF CLOVER PLANT

RESUMÉ: This species includes dear, fuzzy little plants and plants to 8 or 10 inches tall, all with cloverlike leaves that fold together at night. They produce lots of blooms on long, arching stems that stand above the foliage. There are many kinds: *Oxalis hedysaroides rubra,* called 'Firefern,' is 6 inches high and has wine-red ferny foliage and loads of bright yellow flowers; *O. regnellii,* is about 10 inches high and has grass-green leaves and white flowers. These two do better than other kinds when the light available is less than ideal. *O. rubra* is an old-fashioned basket favorite with pink blooms; this is the one I prefer.

RELOCATION: Young plants are charming on a desk or in a nook in a bookcase. As the plant matures, stems lengthen and cascade enough to make oxalis attractive in a small hanging basket or raised on a little pedestal in a window or on a desk corner. The tumble of tiny leaves is especially cozy in a bookcase corner.

SITUATIONS WANTED: A cool room to 70 or 72 degrees with lows at night of 55 degrees is fine. Best light for blooming is in a sunny east or west window in winter, and a few hours of direct sun a few feet back from the window in summer. Fluorescent overheads augmented by some light from a nearby window should be enough to produce bloom. I've seen oxalis bloom under desk lights alone.

SALARY REQUIREMENTS: Allow the soil to begin to dry a little before watering, then drench the plant. One hour later, empty the saucer of excess water. Mist occasionally and air often, especially if temperatures go over 70 degrees. Feed blooming-type plant food and pinch branch tips every few months to keep the plant from growing straggly. Stems on plants short of light contort to reach for more light, and you may have to prune the plant severely to keep it shapely. If the roots crowd the containers, repot in all-purpose soil. Shower when you can, and oxalis will freshen up considerably.

FYI: Oxalis is subject to bugs—mealybugs, aphids, and red spider mites—especially when it's hot.

Paphiopedilum
SLIPPER ORCHIDS

RESUMÉ: Orchid blooms last several weeks, so this isn't a flower you can count on for color on a year-round basis. However, the blooming is an adventure that adds fun and glamor to the office garden. As easy as a begonia, slipper orchids have strap-shaped foliage in plain green or fascinatingly mottled tones, pretty even when the plant is out of bloom. Not quite as glamorous as the corsage orchids, the paphs, as they are called in the trade, resemble wild lady slippers that bloom in northern woodlands. The many varieties have flowers whose colors and markings are extraordinary; blooms may be yellow, red, rose purple, pink, brown, green, white, and are patterned with pencil-thin lines or big or little dots. The blooms rise above the foliage on willowy arching stems. Bloom periods vary with variety; usually there is more than one period a year when the plants are in flower.

RELOCATION: Choose medium-size cachepots of glazed ceramics in colors that complement the bloom colors. *Paphiopedilum maudiae*, an easy plant for beginners, is green and white; a pretty green cachepot will enhance the bloom when it appears and recalls it when there isn't any. Paphs out of bloom look best when combined with foliage plants, such as wandering jew, that do not need direct sunlight. Once blooming, they can be moved to a show spot.

SITUATIONS WANTED: Paphs come from shady tropical forests and will burn in direct sun; four 40-watt fluorescents, close-up, as in a bookcase or wall garden, should be enough to produce flowering; so is a sunless corner of an east or west window. Best temperatures are moderate to warm, 75 to 78 degrees, but paphs require moist air. Lows at night can be to 65 or 60 degrees.

SALARY REQUIREMENTS: Keep the soil evenly moist but don't water until the soil is beginning to feel a little dry. Empty excess saucer water one hour after watering. Mist as often as you can; grow the plants on moist pebble beds to increase moisture. Feed blooming-type plant food summer and winter. If you want to repot or propagate orchids, buy a book on the subject; it is an intricate business though not difficult.

FYI: Cold and dry stale air are bad news.

Pelargonium hortorum
GERANIUM

RESUMÉ: The first indoor plant I ever owned was a geranium cutting, and I've had geraniums ever since. They're very tolerant plants with big, bright blooms in all seasons, sparse or lavish, depending on surrounding conditions. There are miniatures and basket types with waxy foliage, but *Pelargonium hortorum* is the best for offices. These are small bushes, heavily branched, with leaves zoned in light or reddish green in a horseshoe pattern. They are often called zonal geraniums. Flowers are heavy clusters of red, salmon, pink, lavender, or white, some single, some double. Among good indoor bloomers with unusual colors are oranges such as 'Prince of Orange' (blooms are double) and 'Maxime Kovalevski.' There are also violet-colored ones, such as 'Montmartre,' and plants with two-colored blossoms, like 'Apple Blossom,' a favorite with pink-edged white flowers.

RELOCATION: Young geraniums 4 to 8 inches tall are pretty on a sunny desk corner, and a whole row blooming in a window is a first-class cheerer-upper in midwinter. The plants eventually get to be 12 to 24 inches tall, some taller. I prefer pinks and whites in terracotta pots, and the other colors in white plastic containers.

SITUATIONS WANTED: Geraniums like to be cool and need sun to bloom. Days at 70 degrees and nights that go down to 55 degrees are best. Full sun in a south window is ideal in winter; in summer move the plant to a bright west window if you can. Geraniums maintain themselves and bloom in a sunny east or west window, but they may grow leggy and bloom sparsely.

SALARY REQUIREMENTS: Let the soil become dry on the surface before you water, then drench the plant and empty the saucer of excess water an hour later. Mist and air often when temperatures are over 72 degrees. Shower monthly if you can. Pinch back tallest stalks to induce branching; in spring root 6-inch tip cuttings in moist vermiculite or water and pot rooted cuttings in three parts all-purpose soil and one part sand. Feed blooming-type plant food as often as directed.

FYI: Lack of light makes leggy plants.

Phalaenopsis
MOTH ORCHID

RESUMÉ: The moth orchids are like the paphs (*Paphiopedilums*) in several ways: They're as easy to grow as begonias, and many varieties have fascinatingly marked foliage. Generally the moth orchids produce several blooms on each stem, and only some kinds are patterned with stripes and spots. Most varieties are single colors or combinations of two or three colors. *Phalaeonopsis amabilis* is the beautiful moth orchid; on a pendant stalk it produces several white blooms with a yellow crest spotted red on each one. The blooms usually appear between October and January on this kind, but other varieties bloom at other seasons.

RELOCATION: See the suggestions for paphiopedilum (page 157). Phalaenopsis looks great in a wall garden of tropicals year round. Although I sound strict about conditions that this plant needs, New York executive Spencer Douglas grows orchids in his Long Island home very casually—a little misting, good but filtered imperfect light, and they flourish and bloom almost as well as when he grows them in an elaborate greenhouse.

SITUATIONS WANTED: No direct sun, please. Strong light at the side of an east or west window or under fluorescents in a wall garden is fine. Ideal temperatures are on the warm side, to 80 degrees, but there must be lots of moisture in the air: This may be accomplished by growing the plants in a wall or floor garden on a bed of moist pebbles. Nighttime temperatures down to 65 degrees are okay. To help phalaenopsis really bloom at peak, cool the plants for a month in fall or winter by opening a window just a crack; they need four weeks at 55 degrees.

SALARY REQUIREMENTS: Keep the soil evenly moist, but let the surface soil begin to dry out a little before you water. Don't overwater and don't let the plants sit in puddles for any length of time. Empty the saucer one hour after watering. Mist just as often as you can. Feed blooming-type plant food before and during flowering; feed all-purpose plant food the balance of the year.

FYI: Overwatering and hot dry blasts spoil the plant.

Rhipsalidopsis gaertneri
EASTER CACTUS

RESUMÉ: These are jungle cacti. The plants aren't handled like desert cacti, though they're just as fascinating to look at. A cascade of glossy leaflike joints, each tipped with a pendant crimson bloom, identifies an Easter cactus at flowering time. It's a spectacular show and unlike anything else except Christmas cactus (*Schlumbergera bridgesii*), which blooms in November and December, or crab cactus (*Zygocactus truncatus*), which may bloom as early as Thanksgiving and flowers in white, red, scarlet, and orange. All three forms tend to be called any of those common names and have similar needs. I find that Easter cactus is a little more forgiving of mishandling. All three bloom seasonally. The blooms last many weeks; out of bloom, they are handsome foliage plants.

RELOCATION: Young plants are attractive in shiny plastic cubed or round cachepots. Or group three or four on a low pedestal or on a sunny table or windowsill, along with a collection of medium-size cacti and succulents. In bloom the plants demand a show-off place with bright lighting.

SITUATIONS WANTED: This plant is a no-no for offices where lights burn 24 hours a day. To bloom they need long nights of darkness for eight weeks in the fall, starting when summer growth begins to slow. If possible, move to a cool place at that time and allow a rest period with minimal watering and no feeding. The rest of the year, a sunny east or west window or a few feet from a south window are fine. The plant also will adapt to a bright north window and to overhead fluorescents if there is some direct sun from a nearby window. Ideal temperatures are 60 to 70 degrees during the day with nights to 55 degrees except during the rest period.

SALARY REQUIREMENTS: Maintain even moisture and feed blooming-type plant food except during the rest period described above. If the container becomes crowded, repot in African violet soil over 2 inches of pebbles for drainage. An occasional shower helps, but don't wet the plant while in bloom. Air often if you can.

FYI: Night lights inhibit blooming; stale air is unhealthy.

Rosa chinensis minima
PIGMY ROSE
FAIRY ROSE

RESUMÉ: This is an adorable plant 8 to 10 inches high that will produce real but minuscule roses if given four hours of direct sun daily. The pink blooms have a paler eye and are 1½ inches across, double, and darling. *Rosa chinensis minima* 'Oakington Ruby' is a red variety under 12 inches tall with a contrasting zone of white at the base. Dozens of varieties of this and other tiny roses are being sold now by mail order by specialists such as the Sequoia Nursery, 2519 East Noble Street, Visalia, California 93277.

RELOCATION: These roses look loveliest in delicately patterned china cachepots. If you are growing several, set them on a big saucer filled with moist pebbles and place them in a big, deep windowsill. Some types are climbers, and for these you should provide a mini-trellis. Individual plants are charming in a wall garden under grow lights.

SITUATIONS WANTED: Roses need sun or strong light from fluorescents. Use two or three daylight tube fixtures placed 4 to 6 inches above the plant tops and burn them 12 to 16 hours daily. If the roses are in a window, make it a southwest window in fall and winter and an east or west window in summer and spring. Ideal temperatures are 70 degrees for days and down to 55 or 60 degrees at night. Moist, fresh air is essential.

SALARY REQUIREMENTS: Keep the soil evenly damp, not soggy. Mist and air often. About once a month take the plants to the washroom and drench them in the morning and at night. Then let the plants dry out a little more than usual before you resume regular watering. Feed blooming-type plant food every two weeks except in late fall and early winter, when they need a rest period; in late fall, cut back the stalks to 4 or 5 inches and let the plant stay nearly dry in a cool room (40 degrees is ideal); it need not be sunny. In January return the plants to full sunlight and resume regular care. After periods of heavy bloom, pinch back the tips.

FYI: Control aphids and red spider mites with Malathion and Captan following container instructions. For black spot and mildew, use Phaltan and Manzate, also according to directions.

Saintpaulia
AFRICAN VIOLETS

RESUMÉ: African violets are the most popular of all the flowering indoor plants with good reason: They're long-lived—I've known big plants five years old still blooming; they're easy to grow and adaptable to various indoor climates; and they're easy to bring into bloom and reproduce. Plants are 4 to 6 inches tall; the colors range from white through bright showy pinks and blues to lavenders and deep purples. Some are single, some are double, some are edged with frills, some with frills and contrasting colors. The leaves are interesting, too; heart-shaped and hairy, they come in shades from fresh to black green; some are quilted, some frilled, some variegated.

RELOCATION: Young plants will bloom under a desk lamp; groups of plants are charming in big saucers filled with moist perlite or pebbles. My favorite way to use African violets is in a dish garden under fluorescents in a wall or bookcase garden.

SITUATIONS WANTED: African violets bloom in all kinds of light but can take some months to adapt to new situations. Don't keep moving them. Ideal light is probably an east or west window year round, but they'll bloom in a bright north window. A south window is okay in winter but not in summer. They'll also bloom under a desk lamp and under fluorescents in a wall garden. Temperatures can be warm, to 75 or 78 degrees, with nights as low as 65 degrees.

SALARY REQUIREMENTS: Keep the soil evenly moist but not soggy; don't let pots sit in puddles. Be sure to water African violets with lukewarm water; ice-cold water on leaves makes ugly marks. African violets may come back after severe wilting, but you'll lose leaves and blooms. Feed African violet plant food. Remove suckers that grow on stem sides; they inhibit bloom. If containers become crowded, repot in African violet soil over 1 inch pebbles for drainage. Leaf cuttings will root, as described in Chapter 8; pot young plants in African violet soil. Use only plastic pots.

FYI: Hot or cold drafts and soggy soil are bad news.

Spathiphyllum clevelandii
WHITE FLAG

RESUMÉ: This is a tall plant—18 inches to 4 feet high—with big, beautiful, shiny green foliage and white flowers like calla lilies on long willowy stems. A few blooms are produced off and on all year. It is one of the few flowering plants that will thrive in relatively low light, and it is reliable and durable in most indoor climates. Spathiphyllum is from tropical America.

RELOCATION: This belongs in a big handsome cachepot 12 or 13 inches across; a light, colorfully patterned Chinese water urn, for instance, will show off the dark foliage magnificently. Use it as a floor plant or small shrub, or show it off on a low pedestal against a background of airy shrubs or trees. If you need an "instant" plant, cut leaves and keep them in a vase of water. They're long lasting and good-looking.

SITUATIONS WANTED: Ideal light is supplied by a bright north window or a few feet from an east or west window. Overhead fluorescents coupled with light from a bright window, but little or no direct sun, should also be okay. Too much light will turn the leaves yellow and speckle them with brown or black spots; on the other hand, when there's not enough light, the stems will become spindly and the plant will fade away. Temperatures should be between 70 and 78 degrees during the day and not below 65 degrees at night.

SALARY REQUIREMENTS: keep the soil evenly moist but not soggy. Empty saucer an hour after watering. If the leaves wilt, most of them will die, so don't let the plant go dry. Mist often, especially in high temperatures. Feed young plants all-purpose plant food for four months, then switch to blooming-type plant food. Repot only if the container becomes crowded by new growth; use all-purpose potting soil over a couple of inches of pebbles for drainage. Wash the leaves monthly, and if leaf edges brown (usually from overheated dry air or from failure to water the plant), trim the browned parts away with sharp scissors. You can start new plants by dividing and repotting the roots of a parent plant.

FYI: Lighting is a sensitive area; see above. Soggy soil is harmful.

Thunbergia alata
BLACK-EYED-SUSAN VINE

RESUMÉ: This is a 4- to 6-foot climbing plant heavy with heart-shaped leaves and usually grown on a trellis; its big bonus is a profusion of bell-shaped flowers that are creamy yellow or apricot with purple throats. It's a tropical that grows so quickly it is treated as an outdoor annual in many cool areas of the country. Indoors it can be cut back, almost to the ground, after blooming has slowed, and it will begin a new cycle of growth and bloom.

RELOCATION: Place the pot in a handsome massive cachepot (a big polished aluminum cube, for instance) or a neat white plastic cylinder; add a trellis of white lathing, and center the plant at the base of a big empty sunny wall, preferably a white one. The white will reflect additional light and set off the plant. Or, set the pot and its trellis on a low pedestal in a sunny window and think of it as a flowering tree. It can be used as the tall plant at the back of a floor garden, with pedestaled hanging baskets at its feet. It can be the backdrop for a whole garden of flowering plants. Almost any of the plants in this chapter (except orchids and spathiphyllum, which can't take direct sun) should flourish in or near light suitable for *Thunbergia alata.*

SITUATIONS WANTED: Thunbergia needs good light in order to bloom. A spot in a sunny east or west window with several hours of direct sun daily or near a south window is ideal. Temperatures should be moderately warm, 72 to 78 degrees or so, and not below 65 degrees at night. Don't place this plant where the air is stale and dry—it needs moisture and fresh air.

SALARY REQUIREMENTS: Keep the soil evenly moist, but be sure to empty the saucer an hour after watering. In high heats grow thunbergia on a bed of moist pebbles, but make sure the water level of the pebbles is below the pot bottom. Mist the plant often. Feed blooming-type plant food, and if blooming slows, see the instructions noted under Resumé. Repot as needed in African violet soil over 2 inches of pebbles to ensure good drainage.

FYI: Dry air and soggy soil spoil this plant.

7

Putting It All Together: Plant Projects

Single plants spotted here and there on windowsills, file cabinets, and desk tops are nice, but groups of plants together are nicer. Foliage, form, color, branch structure, and growth habit are the characteristics with which the indoor landscaper works. Mix and match them. The gardens in this chapter will give you a notion of what I mean. The key to successful gardens is to choose not only plants that look well together but also plants with similar light needs. Appendix A serves as a quick-reference guide to making these choices. Furthermore, when the garden you are planning is a dish garden, planter, or terrarium, you must choose plants with similar soil needs.

The projects described in this chapter are samples. You may follow them exactly, or if your heart is of a more courageous sort, you may substitute plants according to the above guidelines concerning plant requirements. In any case, remember that the job of planning your office garden is much like your own: There is no substitution for the personal touch.

1 *Ficus benjamina;* **2** *Ficus benjamina* 'Exotica'; **3** *Ficus pumila*

1 *Haworthia;* 2 *Echinocactus grusonii;* 3 *Stapelia melocactus;* 4 *Mammillaria;* 5 *Aeonium haworthii*

Desert Dish Garden

1. *Shopping list:* For this garden you will need a Mexican clay pot or a plant pot saucer 10 to 12 inches across the top by 3 to 5 inches deep; a small bag of small pebbles or small marble chips; a small bag of small charcoal chips; two small bags or one medium of cactus soil; a small bag of beige or white sand— the kind sold for sand paintings or the coarser kind for potting mixtures; a few sheets of old newspaper; and a paper towel or two.

2. *Plants:* Stapelia; melocactus; two varieties of mammillaria (pages 33–34)—one round and one growing in asymmetrical peaks; a haworthia; a golden barrel cactus (*Echinocactus grusonii*); and 'Pinwheel' (*Aeonium haworthii*), a flowerlike succulent.

The following list suggests a few alternate plants that are easy to find. Actually any small cacti or other succulents in 2-inch pots will be compatible in a desert garden: *Opuntia; Echinocereus reichenbachii; Echinocereus rigidissimus; Lobivia; Cephalocereus; Cereus; Rebutia.*

3. Assemble all your materials on spread-out newspaper sheets, along with a small pitcher of water.

4. Layer ½ inch of pebbles or marble chips in the bottom of the pot.

5. Cover the pebbles with a thin layer of charcoal chips.

6. Add cactus soil to within ¾ inch of the container rim. Add enough water to dampen slightly.

7. Group the plants in a circular arrangement the size of the planting pot. Fuss with them, move them around, until you like the way the sizes and shapes balance each other.

8. Working with one plant at a time, knock the pot on the rim of the table to loosen the soil, then slide the rootball out of the pot; if the soil is slightly damp, it will hold together better. Scoop a shallow hole just the size of the rootball in the soil, set the roots into it, and firm the soil gently around the roots. When dealing with prickly cacti, fold a paper napkin into a band and use this to hold the plant while you work with it.

9. When all the plants are in, add just enough tepid water to slightly moisten the soil.

10. Tear a corner hole in the sand bag, and spill just enough sand over the top of the cactus soil to cover it.

11. The right place for this garden is near or in a sunny east, west, or south window. While still young, the cacti will also grow in a fluorescent light garden if grow lights are directly overhead and close. See the description for Cacti and Other Succulents (pages 33–34) for maintenance information.

Dish Garden with Dried Flowers I (Filtered Light Required)

1. *Shopping List:* You will need a bulb pan (a plant pot wider than it is tall) 8 to 10 inches across the top and a terracotta saucer for it; large pebbles or broken bits of clay pot or chunks

1 Honesty; 2 *Polyscias balfouriana pennockii*; 3 *Helichrysum*; 4 *Peperomia sandersii* 'Ripple'; 5 Maranta leuconeura

of sponge to stuff the drainage holes; a small bag of pebbles or marble chips; a medium bag of all-purpose potting soil; several large sheets of old newspaper; and a small fat bottle or short bud vase with a 1-inch mouth. You will also need a fat, short bunch of dried helichrysum (looks like a small chrysanthemum) and six or eight short stalks of honesty (the luminous papery discs called money plant).

2. *Plants:* Maranta (page 48); 'Ripple' (*Peperomia*, page 51); and a young *Polyscias balfouriana pennockii* (pages 111–112). Buy young plants of all three kinds in sizes that fit into 3- or 4-inch pots.

3. Gather all the materials together on spread-out newspaper along with a small pitcher of water. Follow the instructions for potting in item 8 of Soils, Potting, and Repotting (pages 202–203). When placing the rootballs of the plants in the soil, keep them toward the outer edge of the pot, leaving the center free. When the living plants are all potted, firmed into place, and lightly watered, poke a hole in the center of the soil, insert the bottle or bud vase, and arrange a short, fat bouquet of helichrysum and honesty in the center of the dish.

4. Light for this garden can be near an east or west window, but out of direct sun, or under overhead fluorescents with some sun from a nearby window or with additional light from a tall desk lamp burning two 60-watt incandescent lights. Care for the dish is similar to care for the maranta.

5. When the polyscias outgrows its dish, plant it in a pot of its own, and it will be on its way to becoming a shrub for the office; the peperomia and maranta will grow and take up the space vacated by the polyscias.

Dish Garden with Dried Flowers II
(Bright Light Required)

1. *Shopping List:* Same as for the dish garden under filtered light. Instead of the helichrysum and honesty, buy a few short sprays of dried pussy willow and orangy or orange-red statice.

2. *Plants:* Strawberry begonia (*Saxifraga sarmentosa*, page 57), which has small reddish leaves; a miniature *Begonia rex*

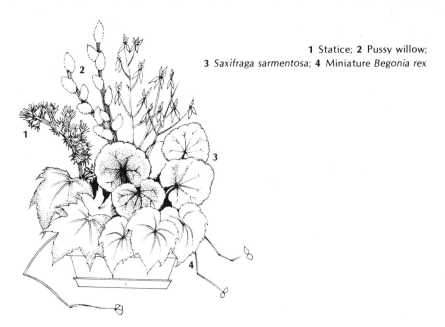

1 Statice; 2 Pussy willow;
3 *Saxifraga sarmentosa*; 4 Miniature *Begonia rex*

(page 32) with silver leaves, and one whose leaves are pink and silver. Buy young plants in 3- to 4-inch pots.

3. Follow planting instructions for the dish garden above.

4. Light for this garden can be in a bright east or west window or several feet from a south window. Overhead fluorescents coupled with a few hours of sun from a nearby window should also be enough for the plant to maintain itself and grow a little. Additional light could also be from two 60-watt bulbs in a tall desk lamp. Care for the garden is similar to care for the strawberry begonia.

Dish Garden on a Pedestal

1. *Shopping List:* Same as for the dish garden under filtered light (pages 169–170), except the pot should be 4 to 6 inches deep, and in addition, you will need a 6- to 8-inch pedestal. Or, dispense with the pedestal and place the garden at the edge of a bookcase shelf, at the corner of a file cabinet, or on a stack of four or five books.

2. *Plants:* Baby false aralia (*Dizygotheca elegantissima*, page 75); hybrid yellow and green croton; purple velvet plant (*Gynura sarmentosa*); creeping fig (*Ficus pumila*, page 130); a brightly variegated *Peperomia caperata* 'Tricolor'; and *Pellionia*

pulchra. This garden cascades at the front and stands tall behind, so choose an 8- or 10-inch-tall skinny croton, a slightly shorter dizygotheca, and a creeping fig that already has several long trailing stems. Croton, gynura, and pellionia aren't the toughest plants around, so I haven't included them among my hundred durables. But they'll do well in this dish garden so long as they aren't overwatered, and most suppliers carry them.

3. Planting instructions are the same as for the two previously mentioned dish gardens. Plant the tall plants first.

4. Light for this garden is somewhere between filtered and bright. A few feet from an east or west window with some overhead fluorescent light is just right. Keep the soil evenly moist but don't overwater.

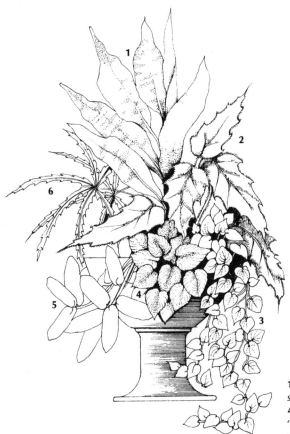

1 Hybrid croton; 2 Gynura
sarmentosa; 3 Ficus pumila;
4 Peperomia caperata
'Tricolor'; 5 Pellionia
pulchra; 6 Dizygotheca
elegantissima

Terrarium with Fresh Flowers

1. *Shopping List:* A small fish tank, 8 to 12 inches long, or a fish bowl or a big brandy snifter with an opening 8 to 12 inches across the top; a glass top cut to fit the container; a small bag of white marble chips; a small bag of small charcoal chips; a small bag of buff-colored coarse sand; a small bag of terrarium soil; big sheets of newspaper; paper towels; several cups of tepid water; bits of moss from the woods; a birch twig or two; and a few small, colored stones.

2. *Plants:* Maidenhair fern (*Adiantum tenerum wrightii*) ; a miniature maple leaf begonia (*Begonia dregei macbethii*) ; a miniature grape ivy (*Cissus striata*) ; a mini creeping fig (*Ficus pumila minima*, page 130) ; a baby bird's-nest fern (*Asplenium nidus*, page 30) ; a spleenwort fern (*Asplenium cristatum*) ; and in a 2-inch pot, a miniature *Begonia richmondensis.* The little begonia will produce tiny pink flowers, but when its out of bloom, you can have flowers by inserting them in an aquapic, a tiny vase with a pointed end and a rubber cap that has a hole in it through which you can insert a small flower stem (see illustration). For blooms use tiny sprigs of geranium or azalea or any blooming office plant or little wild flowers—violets or even plain old dandelions look great featured this way in the mini-world of a terrarium.

You may use any of the following as alternate plants: *Calathea micans* (mini maranta) ; *Chamaedorea elegans* 'Bella' (baby neanthe bella palm) ; *Cryptanthus bivittatus minor*; *Dracaena godseffiana* 'Florida Beauty'; *Hedera helix* 'Manda's Needlepoint' (mini English ivy) ; *Pilea cadierei* (baby aluminum plant) ; *Pilea microphylla* (baby artillery plant) ; *Philodendron sodiroi* (silver-leaved philodendron) ; *Saintpaulia ionantha* (mini African violet) ; *Saxifraga stolonifera* (strawberry geranium).

3. Place a 2- or 3-inch layer of marble chips in the bottom of the container, and shape the terrain into hills and valleys.

4. Cover with a thin layer of charcoal chips.

5. Add sand, making valleys over the "hills" and hills over the "valleys" of marble chips.

6. Add terrarium soil. Increase the depth of the soil at the back of the terrarium to raise taller plants. This lets you feature smaller plants in the foreground.

1 *Begonia dregei macbethii;* **2** *Asplenium nidus;* **3** *Begonia richmondensis;* **4** *Ficus pumila minima;* **5** marble chips; **6** charcoal; **7** sand; **8** soil; **9** *Cissus striata;* **10** *Asplenium nidus*

7. Trace the terrarium bottom on the newspaper, and within it arrange your plants, fussing until you find a charming grouping; or you can follow my arrangement.

8. Planting procedures are the same as for the gardens previously mentioned. Following your planned grouping, set the tallest plants into the soil first and the creepers last. Plant the begonia in its pot.

9. Cover any bare places on the soil with bits of woods moss.

10. Push your aquapic into the soil right to the rim in a spot that will feature the little bloom. But make it somewhere accessible so you can change the water daily and replace the bloom when it fades. Add birch twigs, colored pebbles, or whatever seems appropriate.

11. Add half a cup of tepid water, just enough to moisten the soil.

12. With wet paper towel wrapped around a pencil, wipe the insides of the container clean.

13. Set the glass lid in place and keep it there.

14. Bright daylight or good fluorescent light are ideal for this garden but no direct sun. Two 20-watt fluorescent bulbs, one warm white and one cool white, or one 40-watt fluorescent grow light right over the terrarium are fine, too. They should burn 14 to 16 hours a day if the garden is in a dim corner.

15. A few hours after you have covered the terrarium, beads of water should begin to form on the inside of the glass. When these vanish (every week or ten days usually), add ½ cup of

water. If moisture hasn't formed within 24 hours, add another half cup of water.

16. Keep dead foliage removed to keep the terrarium healthy and trim, and remove any plants that outgrow their spot.

Room-Divider Floor Garden

1. *Shopping List:* One big tin tray 8 feet long by 14 inches wide by 3 inches deep (a tinsmith, an auto body shop, or an air conditioning or heating duct firm probably can make this to order) ; one or two large bags of large marble chips (I can't be specific because makers vary bag sizes) ; nine strips of styro-

1 *Dracaena massangeana;* 2 *Dracaena marginata;* 3 *Dracaena deremensis warneckei;* 4 tray with pebbles; 5 styrofoam strips

foam 12 inches long by 2 inches wide by about 1 to 2 inches high; water enough to half fill the tray.

2. *Plants:* Two *Dracaena fragrans massangeana* (page 106) 5 to 6 feet tall; one *Dracaena marginata* (page 106) 4 feet tall and one 5 feet tall; one *Dracaena deremensis warneckei* (pages 76–77) 1½ feet tall and one 2½ feet tall. Have the plants repotted by the supplier in big, clean terracotta containers.

3. Set the tray in place, and under it space the styrofoam strips every 8 inches. The strips will let enough air get under the tray to dry the condensation that forms on hot days. Half fill the tray with pebbles, and add enough water to bring the level just below but not touching pot bottoms.

4. Arrange the plants as shown in the sketch.

5. This garden needs filtered light; a good location is several feet from a bright east or west window or under bright fluorescent overheads. For maintenance, see the instructions for handling *Dracaena fragrans massangeana* (page 106).

Room Divider for a Three-Drawer File Cabinet

1. *Shopping List:* For a cabinet whose dimensions are 27 inches long by 14 inches wide (standard) you will need a tray 25 by 14 by 2 inches deep; four strips of styrofoam 12 inches long by 2 inches wide by 1 inch high; and a medium bag of small pebbles or marble chips. To hang the creeping fig, you will also need a ceiling hook, a molly plug big enough to take it, and clear nylon fishing line 20- to 40-pound test. The basket hangs low enough in this arrangement to water easily so you don't need a pulley arrangement.

2. *Plants:* A fig tree (*Ficus benjamina*, page 107) 3 or 4 feet tall; one *F. diversifolia* (page 46); one mature creeping fig (*F. pumila*, page 130) in a hanging basket; one *F. benjamina* 'Exotica' (page 107) 2 to 3 feet tall.

3. Set the tray on styrofoam strips, half fill the tray with pebbles, add water to just below pot bottoms.

4. Display the plants as illustrated.

5. Screw the molly plug into the ceiling, screw the hook end into it, tie the nylon line to the hook.

6. Replace the basket wires with nylon line and tie the ceiling line to it.

7. Light and care of ficuses are discussed in preceding chapters; see pages suggested above.

1 *Ficus benjamina;* 2 *Ficus pumila;* 3 *Ficus benjamina* 'Exotica'; 4 *Ficus diversifolia*

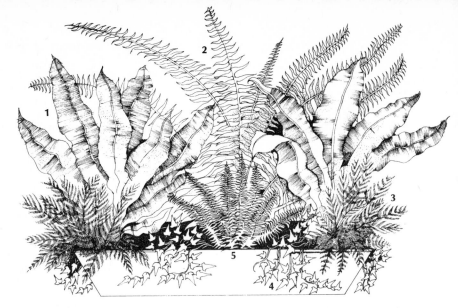

1 *Asplenium nidus;* 2 *Nephrolepis exaltata bostoniensis;* 3 *Davallia fejeensis;* 4 *Hedera helix;* 5 *Nephrolepsis exaltata* 'Fluffy Ruffles'

Fern Planter

1. *Shopping List:* There are ready-made planters in standard sizes, 10 or 12 inches deep by 10 or 12 inches tall, and of average sill length, 3 to 4 feet long. These are mounted on sturdy legs. You can also hire a carpenter to make one for you any length or height your location requires. Depth and width should be 12 inches deep by 12 inches wide. To fill a planter 6 feet long, 12 inches wide, and 12 inches deep, buy about 6 cubic feet of all-purpose soil and enough pebbles to create 2 inches of drainage at the bottom of the planter.

2. *Plants:* The sketch includes a big Boston fern (*Nephrolepis exaltata bostoniensis,* page 49) and its smaller variety, 'Fluffy Ruffles'; two bird's-nest ferns (*Asplenium nidus,* page 30); and two *Davallia fejeensis* (page 42). Four English ivies (*Hedera helix* 'Pinoak) creep forward from between the ferns and tumble over the planter sides.

Alternate plants: *Davallia fejeensis plumosa;* adiantum; *Nephrolepis exaltata* 'Rooseveltii'; *N. e.* 'Massii'; *N. e.* 'Verona'; *N. e.* 'Whitmanii'; *N. e.* 'Norwoodii'; *Cyrotomium falcatum;* *Hedera helix* 'Merion Beauty.'

3. Line the planter with 2 inches of pebbles and fill it with all-purpose soil to within 1½ inches of the rim. Potting procedures are the same as for the desert dish garden, item 8, page 169. Set the big Boston fern in place first, the bird's-nest ferns next, davallia next, and then center 'Fluffy Ruffles' just in front of the big Boston fern. Poke English ivy plants in between the bigger plants and draw the stems forward so they tumble over the planter top.

4. The right light for this planter is filtered, and the planter wants a coolish room and lots of misting. Keep the soil evenly moist. For detailed maintenance suggestions, look up any of the pages listed with the suggested ferns.

Water Garden

1. *Shopping List:* You can buy a push-botton hydroponic unit that grows plants in water for about $20 or $30, or for much less, you can recreate the water garden sketched here. Buy three bake trays 18 by 12 inches by 2 inches deep; one small bag of small pebbles; three clay bulb pans 8 inches across the top; two clay bulb pans 6 inches across the top; one standard-shape clay

1 *Nephrolepsis exalta bostoniensis;* 2 *Dieffenbachia;* 3 *Aglaonema;* 4 *Cyperus alternifolius*

pot 6 inches across the top; polyurethane and a paintbrush; and a bit of fiberglass or fine sponge.

2. *Plants:* Tip cuttings or root divisions of umbrella plant (*Cyperus alternifolius*, page 40), Chinese evergreen (*Aglaonema*, page 26), and dumbcane (*Dieffenbachia*, page 74). The fourth plant, a young Boston fern (*Nephrolepis exaltata bostoniensis*) should be potted in a standard 6-inch clay container.

Alternate plants can be any of those noted in Chapters 2–6 that will grow for long periods in water. To name a few: *Coleus* species; *Dracaena fragrans; Nephthytis; Philodendron selloum; Tradescantia* species.

3. Stuff the drainage holes in the bulb pans with a bit of fiberglass or fine sponge. With the paintbrush, apply several coats of polyurethane to the inside of the bulb pans. Three to four coats will waterproof them. Sprinkle a layer of pebbles on the tray. Fill the bulb pan with tepid water, and place in them the tip cuttings or root divisions of the plants suggested or any others you may have or prefer. Arrange the pots as shown in the sketch. The fern sits on the standard-shape pot which has been upended to make a pedestal.

4. Filtered light is suitable for the garden shown. Check the water in the bulb pans every week or so to make sure it isn't below the level of the cuttings. Mondays and Thursdays, check the fern. It should be kept evenly moist. If you keep ¼ inch of water in the tray, it will help keep the air moist around the fern and will cut down on the need to mist.

Corner Floor Garden with Seasonal Flowers

1. *Shopping List:* Groups of plants set on the floor are easiest to handle and most successful when they are growing on a bed of moist pebbles. It keeps the air humid around the plants and creates visual harmony and unity. The plan here is for a corner garden near a bright window and growing in a big floor tray. The tray can be custom made by a carpenter or can be an assembly of three planting trays on rollers (commercial units that retail at something under $100 each). If you have yours custom made, make sure that the depth is a full 6 to 8 inches and that it has a watertight tin liner. Every 8 inches under the tray,

1 *Chamaedorea erumpens;* **2** *Polyscias balfouriana;* **3** Azaleas;
4 *Dizygotheca elegantissima*

place styrofoam strips 1 to 2 inches wide and 2 inches short of
the tray so they won't show. This allows just enough air circulation under the tray to dry condensation on the tray bottom. In
addition to a tray and liner, you will need a lot of marble chips
—one or two of the largest bag sizes.

2. *Plants:* 5- to 6-foot bamboo palm (*Chamaedorea erumpens,*
pages 102–103), or buy a 3- to 4-foot bamboo palm and set it on a
2- or 3-foot pedestal. The pedestal could be a clay pipe or any
pottery piece that can stand in moist pebbles or just a great big
chunk of tree trunk; a 4- to 5-foot false aralia (*Dizygotheca
elegantissima,* page 75) ; a *Polyscias balfouriana* (pages 111–112)

2 to 4 feet tall; and two or three pots of seasonal flowers in bloom: For instance, in spring buy pink azalea or big pots of blue hyacinth bulbs; in fall, chrysanthemums; and poinsettias at Christmas. Between the two false aralias, you can display tall vases of cut flowers or flowering branches such as forsythea and Japanese cherry blossoms, both available in late winter and early spring.

Alternate plants: Use a *Ficus benjamina* (page 107) instead of the tall bamboo palm; 2- or 3-foot *Ficus benjamina exotica* (page 107) instead of the false aralia, and big pots of creeping fig (*Ficus pumila*, page 130) raised on upturned standard clay pots instead of the *Polyscias balfouriana*. The illustration at the beginning of this chapter (page 167) will give you an idea of how this grouping will look. Any seasonal flowers will be lovely in this dainty cascade of leaves.

3. Established beside an east, west, or south window, this garden should get all the light it needs. It could also flourish under two or three 8-foot fluorescent light tracks with six to nine fixtures. See Light for the Office Garden section of Chapter 8. The garden should require watering (except for seasonal flowers) only weekly or every ten days.

Bookcase Garden

1. *Shopping List:* A tin tray 2 inches deep, 1 inch less wide than your bookcase shelf, and whatever length your bookcase is. You can have one custom made or put side by side several tin bake trays 18 by 12 inches by 2 inches deep or pyrex bake trays 15 by 9 inches by 2 inches deep. To help you plan: A tray 18 by 12 inches accommodates about three small African violets, two deep—in other words, five or six plants, depending on the spread of their leaves. A 15-by-9-inch tray accommodates four to six miniature rex begonias or wax begonias. You will also need several bags of small pebbles or marble chips; one small bag of pebbles is enough for one 15-by-9-inch tray. For light, buy two 20-watt grow lights, one warm white, one cool white, in a reflector fixture. Add a timer, a strip of molding to match the height and length of the tray rim, and hammer and nails for attaching the molding to the bookcase.

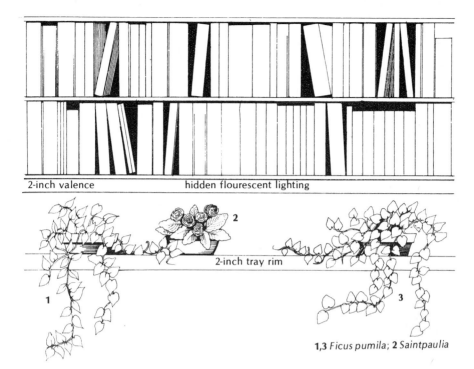

2-inch valence   hidden flourescent lighting

2-inch tray rim

1,3 *Ficus pumila;* **2** *Saintpaulia*

2. *Plants:* African violets (*Saintpaulia*, page 162) in assorted blues, some variegated; baby coleus (keep it pinched back!) in pale rose, white and green variegations; strawberry begonia (*Saxifraga sarmentosa*, page 57); and baby browallia (page 151), blooming in violet blue to trail over the corners.

Alternate plants: You can do this garden primarily in pink by substituting pink African violets for blue and replacing the browallia by tiny creeping fig (*Ficus pumila*, page 130), or small-leaved English ivy (*Hedera helix*, page 131), such as 'Glacier,' which is variegated green, white, and pink.

3. Install the lights, fix the molding at the edge of the bookcase, set the tray in place half filled with marble chips or pebbles, and add water to just below the pot bottoms. Set your plants on the tray in a pleasing arrangement, with the strawberry begonia and browallia near the front corners and the coleus at the back. Set the timer to burn 15 hours daily and turn on the lights. If the little garden receives quite a lot of light from other sources—windows, desk lamps—its own garden lights may need to burn fewer hours. Watch new plant growth and change the

light timer if necessary. See the section on Light for the Office Garden in Chapter 8.

4. These plants will be growing and blooming, so follow container instructions for feeding.

Three-Shelf Wall Garden

1. *Shopping List:* The principle of this wall garden plan, 8 feet 6 inches long, is the same as for the bookshelf garden previously described. You can have a tin tray made to any dimensions you like, or you can place side by side trays of the sort recommended for the bookcase garden. You will also need valances of wood or plywood (dimensions as shown on the design sketch). The top-shelf garden takes four 20-watt fluorescent lights and so does the second. The bottom tier, which offers more growing room, takes four 40-watt fluorescent fixtures. In addition, you will need a timer to control the lights.

2. *Plants:* Any of these is suitable: African violets, azaleas (seasonal), begonias, davallia, cacti and other succulents, calceolaria (seasonal), Chinese evergreen, coleus, coralberry, cycla-

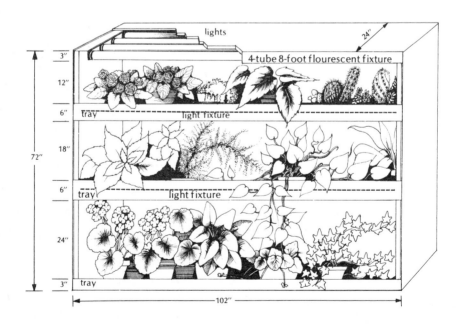

men, dracaena ('Florida Beauty'), echeveria, ferns, gardenia (seasonal), geranium, grape ivy, haworthia, hibiscus, *Hoya carnosa*, impatiens, English ivy, German ivy, jade plant, kalanchoe, orchids, oxalis, pellionia, peperomia, philodendron (young plants), piggyback plant, pilea, polyscias (small plants), pothos, prayer plant, and miniature rose.

3. The procedure for putting this garden together is the same as for putting together a bookcase garden, page 182–184. Lights should burn 12 to 15 hours a day; adjust the time according to plant responses. Choose low plants for the top shelves since the light is closer, and choose plants that can enjoy the cooler air for the lowest shelf, since this will be close to the floor.

Mini-Greenhouse

1. *Shopping List:* Do you have a sunny window ruined for plants in winter by an ugly little radiator or heat convector? Turn it into a mini-greenhouse and grow roses there. You will need one wooden plank 1 to 2 inches thick, the same size and color as the radiator; a tray 1 inch narrower than the plank, 2 to 3 inches deep, or use several glass bake trays; several bags of small pebbles.

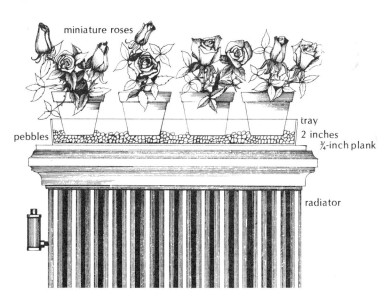

2. *Plants:* A 15-inch tray will take four miniature roses comfortably or five if they are real minis.

Alternate plants: Any of the sun-loving plants described in this book that respond well to humidity will flourish in a south window. For a bright but sunless window you might choose to grow the orchids, paphiopedilum and phalaenopsis, in this mini-greenhouse.

3. Set the plank on top of the radiator. Place the tray on top, half fill it with pebbles, and add water to just below plant pot rims. Set the plants on the pebbles.

4. Heat below the pebbles makes the water in the tray evaporate quickly and keeps the air around the plants constantly humid—a real indoor greenhouse. The only thing you have to worry about is keeping the tray filled with water. If it runs out, the plants could bake. Also be wary of plants whose branches reach out beyond the sides of the plank; if hot blasts of air from the radiator below touch them, leaves touched will curl up and die. Weekends are specially tricky. If the heat stays on all weekend and the water evaporates fast, best weekend the plants on a sunny desk.

Ivy Topiary

1. *Shopping List:* A circular topiary frame 12 inches across (these are sold by some florists and garden supply centers) ; a box of twist ties, or a ball of dark green wool; plant scissors.

2. *Plants:* English ivy (*Hedera helix*, page 131). You'll find suitable ones at summer's end at a florist. Choose one with stems 24 to 30 inches long.

Alternate plants: Creeping fig (*Ficus pumila*, page 130) ; or wax plant (*Hoya carnosa*, page 132).

3. Insert the prong ends of the topiary wire into the soil on either side of the plant. Tie the two longest plant stems gently into place around the wire with twist ties or wool. Work the other long stems around the wire in a way that fills empty spaces. Snip off any short stems that spoil the symmetry of the topiary. As the plant grows, snip off tips of new branches to keep growth

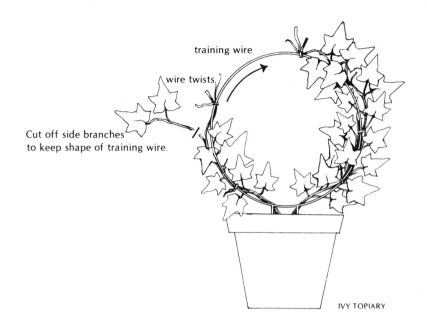

training wire

wire twists

Cut off side branches
to keep shape of training wire.

IVY TOPIARY

symmetrical or work them into the existing circle of leaves. After the plant has been tied, mist it several times a day and remove any dead leaves or branches as they appear.

4. For light and care of the ivy topiary, see *Hedera helix* (page 131).

8

Fact Sheet: Maintaining the Office Garden

The more you know about plants, the more fun they are. The more care you give them, the more satisfaction you'll have in the way they look. You get to love a plant as you get to love a puppy—by caring for it. The preceding chapters describe the needs and foibles of the office indestructibles—90 percent of what you want to know to keep them going. Here's a recap, along with specifics, for the 10 percent not included in previous pages.

Understanding Plant Names

1. The biggest division among plants is the plant families: Liliaceae, Orchidaceae, for example. These words mean Lily family and Orchid family.

2. Each plant family includes many different genera (genus is singular). The Lily family includes the genera *Tulipa*, *Pleomele*, and *Yucca*, among others.

3. Included in each genus are many species: *Pleomele reflexa* is one of the Pleomeles.

4. Included in each species are many varieties: *Pleomele reflexa variegata* is commonly called 'Song of India.'

6. When you see a common name in quotes, like 'Song of India,' it means that variety is the only pleomele bearing that name. When you see a common name without quotes and lower-cased, like wax begonia, that means many varieties are called that name. 'Charm' is a named variety of wax begonia.

Purchasing

1. Good-looking, cut-rate plants are risky buys. White fly may be the least of the ills that comes with such plants.

2. Conscientious dealers acclimatize their plants before selling them. These are sometimes referred to as "Shade grown." Since it takes time and money to acclimatize plants, they are more expensive.

3. Large southern growing areas are California, Texas, and Florida. Florida growers have lower costs because of their climate, so Florida plants (if they reach your area) may be less expensive.

4. Plants browning and withering away on open carts in five-and-dime stores and supermarkets aren't good buys. Even if the one you select looks healthy, they've probably all been neglected.

5. Plants sold in clear plastic cartons in dime stores or supermarkets generally are more costly than those sold without a covering, but less costly than those at florists, and are usually in pretty good shape. Often, they are guaranteed for 30 days.

6. A plant standing in exhaust fumes, heat or cold, on the sidewalk outside a plant shop may have suffered damage. Choose from the plants inside the store. Try to make sure that the one you choose wasn't standing outside yesterday.

7. When buying rapid growers, like wandering jew, choose semimature plants. When buying staked plants, like philodendron, choose plants that haven't reached the top of their stakes.

Helping Plants to Acclimatize

1. New growth is a sure sign that a plant is doing well and has acclimated to its new home.

2. Some plants won't do anything but sulk for several months after a move: African violets, for instance. Be patient!

3. Some plants (ficuses, for instance, and plants shipped or packaged in closed containers) drop lots of leaves when they move.

4. As long as a plant is maintaining itself, it probably is all right, especially if light is lower than instructions specify. In less light plants maintain themselves but can't grow.

5. Misting several times a day helps new plants adjust. Airing the room frequently helps, too. They've come from airy, moist greenhouses or plant shops, and the more you can imitate their recent surroundings, the more quickly they'll adapt. You can overmist too. Don't mist blooms.

6. Don't move plants around a lot. They must acclimate to each change you make. However, if a plant isn't adjusting, you can try a new locale. Or better yet, adjust the existing locale by improving existing conditions.

7. Plants adjust to less-than-ideal conditions. For instance, if you want to grow ferns, which prefer filtered light, in a bright window, move them gradually toward the window over a period of months.

Light for the Office Garden

1. Light is more or less equal *near* east, *near* west, *right in* a north, or *several feet* from a south window.

2. Sun streaming through a south window is as powerful a *few feet* (say 2 or 3) from the window as it is right in front of the window.

3. Summer window light is considerably stronger than window light in winter and can burn plants (such as African violets) that did well there during other seasons.

4. Big open offices with both window and overhead fluorescent light provide light strong enough for most of the plants in this book.

5. If plants aren't getting enough light, they'll tell you: Spindly stems, leaves coming in widely spaced on the stems, and paling leaf colors are signs of lack of light. Also, falling leaves for some plants (ficuses, in particular) is another indication of insufficient light.

Geranium with spindly stems

6. You can improve light by moving the plant closer to a window; raising the plant to a partition, a room divider, a bookcase, a file cabinet top, a pedestal (from a higher location it will get more light from the various sources supplying the room);

by burning existing lights longer (put them on a timer and let them burn four or six hours after work). Lights on a timer that turn on and off while the staff is home can be the main supply source for big plants that can then rest during the day in a dimmer interior. Sometimes just raising venetian blinds after work hours will give enough additional light from sunset and sunrise. Give plants struggling with too little light occasional vacations by moving them into a sunny spot when the occupant of a south-facing office is away or on holiday. Reverse these suggestions and you can lessen the light for plants that are getting too much.

7. You also can increase light by adding individual plant spotlights, floodlights, ordinary lamp lights, or fluorescent lights. Start by adding one light; if spindly growth shows this is insufficient, add two.

8. Lights divide into two categories for our purposes: incandescent (ordinary) bulbs and fluorescents (tubes). There are lights called "grow lights" sold in each category.

9. Plants growing under the kinds of lights called "warm" (this includes ordinary incandescent lamplights) grow slowly; they are wide, stubby, and heavily foliaged. Plants growing under the kind of lights called "cool" (fluorescents) grow quickly but may be leggy. Lights sold as "grow" or "plant" lights in either fluorescent tubes or incandescent bulbs generally have been constructed in such a way that they provide both warm and cool light benefits to the plants. Most modern offices combine both warm and cool fluorescent lights in their overhead ceiling illumination, and that's good for most plants.

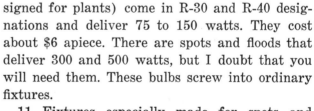

10. Spotlights (incandescents especially designed for plants) come in R-30 and R-40 designations and deliver 75 to 150 watts. They cost about $6 apiece. There are spots and floods that deliver 300 and 500 watts, but I doubt that you will need them. These bulbs screw into ordinary fixtures.

11. Fixtures especially made for spots and floods are sold for use on floors; some insulated kinds are offered for use in tray gardens, and there are extendable fixtures like floor lamps and fixtures that screw into screens, partitions, etc.

floor spot

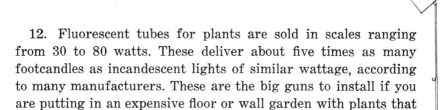

12. Fluorescent tubes for plants are sold in scales ranging from 30 to 80 watts. These deliver about five times as many footcandles as incandescent lights of similar wattage, according to many manufacturers. These are the big guns to install if you are putting in an expensive floor or wall garden with plants that need a lot of light. I suggest you hire a pro to make the installation and choose the plants.

13. There are also 20-watt fluorescent grow or plant lights for use in reflectors (place over tray gardens and bookcase gardens). A single 20-watt tube (equals 100-watt incandescent) does well by my wandering jew and syngonium; it burns 24 hours a day. (The wandering jew, however, is climbing up the

extendable spotligh

back wall, telling me it would like more light). Raising or lowering the height of the tubes, adding another tube, or burning tubes for longer or shorter periods are ways you can adjust this kind of lighting. Complete grow light, reflector, and tray installations are sold together, and these include specific instructions for handling the lights.

14. A track system (looks rather like a traverse rod for a curtain) is the correct choice of lighting if you are installing an expensive garden in a dimly lighted space. These are 4 to 8 feet long, hold one to four lamps, and can be hooked to dimmers, timers, and other gadgetry that make gardening indoors easier. A track system for a floor or wall garden 9 feet long by 3 or 4 feet wide could cost as little as $150. A light system with eight tracks, 24 lights, timers, the works, could cost over $1,000.

track lights

15. To give you any more information about lights would be to plunge us both into confusion of footcandles, angstroms—information you don't need unless you are going to go into the plant business. Read and follow the instructions that come with the grow lights.

Watering and Humidifying

1. Overwatering accounts for more plant deaths than underwatering—or anything else for that matter.

2. Lack of humidity and fresh air is responsible for the failure of some plants to adjust to new surroundings.

3. Many plants brown leaf edges when there is less than 20 percent humidity in the room. In greenhouses, humidity is 30 to 60 percent. In the average hot office, it is about 5 percent.

4. To get an accurate gauge of the humidity in your office, use a hygrometer.

humidifier

5. If humidity in your office registers at below 20 percent, and you have more than five or six plants, consider installing a humidifier (good for people, too). Costs start at about $17 and go soaring up. Choose the kind that spits cool mist, not hot steam.

6. If you cannot have a humidifier, grow your plants—especially those plants noted for needing moisture in the air—on beds of moist pebbles and mist daily. In summer, weekly misting may be enough.

7. If there are humidifiers, mist twice weekly. In summer, skip misting. If windows are open, stop the humidifiers but mist weekly unless the air is humid.

8. Mist the air *around* the plants, not the leaves.

9. Misters cost about $25 for battery-powered kinds, which are especially useful when there are tall trees and high-up hanging baskets. Hand-operated misters cost between $2 and $10. My favorite is a one-quart plastic bottle operated by a pistollike trigger.

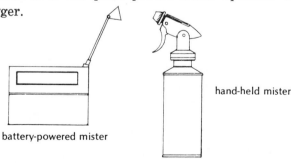

hand-held mister

battery-powered mister

10. When making a pebble bed for a plant, half fill the saucer or tray with pebbles. You can use perlite (light white stuff used to lighten soil) or small river-washed pebbles (buff colored) or white or colored pebbles sold for fish tanks or big beautiful polished black stones used for Japanese gardens (for under trees and other large plants) or marble chips.

 moist pebble bed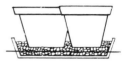

11. Keep the water level in the pebbles below pot bottoms; be very particular about this for plants whose soil is to be kept evenly moist.

12. Pebble beds are kept only partially filled by drain off from watering of pots; check weekly and add water if level of water is less than 1/4 inch.

13. To remove water from a pebble bed, use a small cup or an oven baster.

14. Airing the room by opening doors, windows, or using the air conditioner to draw in outside air raises humidity in winter.

15. Showering small plants monthly humidifies and refreshes them. Set the plant in the washroom sink and gently pour tepid water over the leaves' surfaces.

16. Every month or at least twice a year (before and after the winter heating goes on) sponge the leaves of big plants to clean them. I work with soft paper towels and a big bowl of tepid water. If I can, I dip the leaves into the bowl and really clean them. For palms use a feather duster to clean the fronds.

17. For watering purposes, plants divide into three categories: those kept evenly moist; those kept quite moist; and those whose surface soil should be allowed to dry a little between waterings.

18. Elvin McDonald worked out the best description I know of "evenly moist." He describes it as the way a sponge is when it is wet enough to give out a few drops of water if you squeeze it lightly. If you keep this in mind, you can figure out what "quite moist" and "dry a little" mean.

19. It is a poor idea to let any plant get dust-bowl dry, even plants "resting" in dark closets. Water these about once a month.

20. Plants to be kept quite moist and those to be kept evenly

moist generally need a modest amount of water at each watering; but water fairly often.

21. Plants to be allowed to dry a little between waterings usually are watered less often but should be drenched when watered: Add water until it seeps into the saucer.

22. *Always* empty saucer one hour after watering.

23. Moisture-measuring devices are beginning to flood the market: Some cost a little, others are very expensive. Test them before you confide your watering patterns to them. They can't replace your practiced evaluation of a plant's need.

24. Wicks meant for watering of plants while you are away may be inefficient; anyway, why bother? Surely you have neighbors who can do the watering while you're gone.

25. Three-inch pots can dry in just hours in a overheated office.

26. Five- and 6-inch pots generally need watering once weekly —or twice at most.

27. Pots 6 to 11 inches across the top probably need watering once a week.

28. Pots 12 to 19 inches across the top probably need watering every ten days.

29. Watering patterns change; when winter heating units go on, plants need watering more often. The same applies during growth seasons, early spring and mid-spring.

30. Code plants with colored stickers to indicate watering patterns. See information on garden logs and labels in the Maintenance, Grooming, and Vacations section, pages 209–211. That makes it easy for friends to water for you.

31. Top watering means watering the top of the soil until water seeps into the saucer; bottom watering means filling the saucer with water and letting the plant absorb the water.

32. Bottom watering is indicated for plants whose leaves spot easily (African violets, for instance). Except, as long as the water isn't cold, I find they don't spot even when wetted, unless sun is shining directly on them.

33. If possible, water plants in the morning when there are long hours of light ahead.

34. Take the time to water intelligently; watering is the plant's happy hour of the week. Don't stint your attention.

35. Among watering equipment, there's not a confusion of choices. Watering cans come in sizes up to 8 quarts. Four- to

6-quart cans filled with water are as much as I can handle comfortably, especially when reaching high up. When there are lots of plants, the best method is to buy a big outdoor watering can and use it to fill a small 2- to 4-quart indoor can—the one you use for watering.

36. *Always* use tepid water.

Air and Temperature

1. Most of the plants in this book like temperatures between 68 and 75 degrees, just like you.

2. Most plants enjoy a nighttime drop in temperature—7 to 10 degrees—but can manage without. Most can take occasional drops to 50 degrees. You can lower temperatures at night by opening the window a crack—1/2 inch—before you leave work.

3. Plants can take higher heats in summer, especially if there is lots of fresh air available.

4. Most plants don't mind air conditioning unless it is blasting cold air right on them.

5. Most plants can't stand being near hot air convectors, especially if it is blowing heat at them.

6. You can lower temperatures in an overheated office by opening windows and doors, by cracking (raise a fraction) windows, or by using the air conditioner to draw cool air from the outdoors.

7. Plants need fresh air: If you can, air the room daily. (See previous item.)

8. Few plants can flourish in dead-air spaces; corners have little air and so do the centers of in-curving partitions.

9. Many plants wither in hot or cold drafts.

10. Drafts occur in the air paths between doors and windows that face each other.

11. Frequently traveled corridors, even within big open rooms, generally have hidden drafts.

Feeding

1. There are two basic kinds of plant food: food for foliage plants or all-purpose plant food and food for blooming plants

or African violet plant food. Some are liquids and some are powders; both are added to the watering can. Sticks of fertilizers, pellets, and such come and go. I don't recommend them.

2. Some plant foods are formulated to be given every time you water. Others are meant for periodic feeding.

3. Most plant foods include chemicals: They build up in soils. Fertilizer buildup causes tissue damage, browning leaf tips, leaf drop, and mutation of growth.

4. If you suspect fertilizer buildup, flush the soil as described for *Rosa chinensis minima* (page 161).

5. When using plant food meant to be administered every couple of weeks or so, as a rule of thumb, I recommend that you feed plants half as often as package instructions recommend. For foods meant to be administered with each watering, use half as much as package directs.

6. Feed flowering plants and rapid growers, like the vines, more often than slow-growing foliage plants.

7. Periods when plants really need food are when they are growing rapidly. A plant in less than ideal light may be maintaining itself but not growing. It needs almost no food except one feeding in early, mid, and late spring, and add one more in the fall.

8. Plant foods vary in composition. By changing brands every four to six months, you probably improve the plant's diet.

9. When you want plants to grow foliage and stems rapidly, choose a 5–10–5 composition (those numbers appear on plant food labels). For older foliage plants, choose a 7–6–19 mixture to promote health and foliage.

10. If you have been feeding all-purpose food to promote stem growth for flowering plants, switch to a blooming-type plant food several weeks (six to eight) before the plant is due to come into a blooming cycle. For most plants, that's early spring.

11. When you repot a plant (see below), you are in fact giving it a whole new batch of food, so don't feed it until it has been growing well for two months.

Soils, Potting, and Repotting

1. Bagged plant soils are offered in four compositions: cactus mixes, blooming (African violet) mixes, all-purpose (foliage) mixes, and terrarium mixes.

2. Garden supply centers also sell bagged sand and bagged humus. Adding sand improves drainage and is recommended for some plants in the preceding chapters. Adding humus increases moisture retention and is also indicated for some plants in preceding chapters.

3. To add one part sand to three parts all-purpose soil means to add one third as much sand as you have soil. A good way to measure is with a big 4-quart cup, but anything will do; just measure out three measures of whatever soil you are using, then measure out, add, and mix in one part of sand, humus, or whatever has been indicated.

4. Garden supply centers also sell small gravel. Lay gravel in the bottom of pots to improve drainage. You surely know by now that waterlogged, soggy soil is hazardous for everything but bog plants! As a rule of thumb, a single layer of pebbles is enough for a 3-inch pot; 1 or 2 inches of gravel are suitable for pots in larger sizes. For a great big pot, 19 inches, for instance, you could add 3 to 4 inches of gravel.

5. Plants need potting or repotting when one of the following conditions exist:

a. They are newly rooted babies growing in moist vermiculite or water.

b. The plants are pot-bound. Symptoms are roots growing through drainage holes; stems jammed right against the pot sides; all-around slow-down in what was good growth. To check, knock the pot gently against a hard surface to loosen the soil, then spread your fingers across the top around the stems, and turn the pot upside down. The root ball will slide out of the pot. If roots are wound round and round the outside of the root ball (soil), it is pot-bound.

c. Possible fertilizer buildup. See symptoms described under item 3, Feeding, pages 199–200.

d. When you've just bought plants and the pots seem small in proportion to the stems and branches or when soil of newly purchased plants is hard or showing green moss on top. It is a very good idea to repot everything you buy when plant containers are under 4 inches.

6. Repotting usually results in a flurry of growth within weeks.

7. Plants in big pots, 11 inches and up across the top, are very difficult to repot. They should be repotted every three or four years. See discussion on top dressing and repotting big plants in Chapter 4, pages 93–94.

8. To pot and repot a plant:

a. Choose a new container 1 or 2 inches larger all around than the one the plant now occupies.

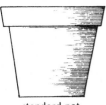

b. Choose terracotta pots for plants requiring very good drainage and which like to dry a little between waterings; choose plastic pots for other plants, particularly African violets and plants whose tender stems may be damaged by roughness of terracotta pot edges.

standard pot

bulb pan

c. Line pots with gravel. See item 4 of this section. Pots over 3 inches have large drainage holes; block these with broken bits of terracotta or torn-up moss, bits of sponge, or anything porous that lets water run through but blocks gravel and soil.

d. Add soil (see items 1, 2, 3 of this section) to a level that will bring the top of the plant's root ball ½ inch (for plants in pots under 4 inches) to 2 inches (plants in 11- or more inch pots) below the top of the pot rim. This leaves space to hold water and makes it easier to water.

e. Remove the plant from its container (see item 5). With a pencil or your finger, gently work the wound-around roots free from the outside of the root ball.

f. Place the root ball on top of the soil in the exact center of the pot. Add soil, forcing it gently down around the sides, until it is even with the top of the root ball.

g. Water the plant well and let it drain; add more soil if needed to bring the soil level back to the top of the root ball. Water once more; mist the leaves.

h. Set the plant in modest light for three days to recover, then return it to its original location.

i. Don't feed the plant until it starts growing well again. Potting soils contain fertilizers and are, in fact, fresh food.

single stem plant (*Pelargonium hortorum*)

j. Root balls of some plants include a single stem from which roots grow. Geranium (*Pelargonium*) is typical. Other plants (spider plant [*Chlorophytum comosum*], for instance) grow by multiplying, creating separate new plants called offsets. When repotting one of the latter, you can remove some of the offsets and use these to start new plants. A single offset potted usually looks lonely; pot up five or six to make a better-looking plant.

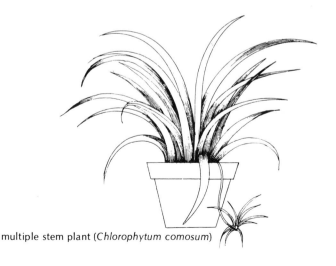

multiple stem plant (*Chlorophytum comosum*)

Pinching and Pruning

1. Pinching is when you snip out the tiny new growth at the end of a stem. (I use my fingernails.)

2. Pruning is when you cut away several inches of a stem or a whole branch. Use a sharp knife, an X-acto knife, or a safety razor for tender growth; use pruning shears for woody growth.

3. The purpose of pinching is generally to force the plant to branch out at its base. Pruning may be done for that reason, but it also is a technique used to shape plants like avocados (*Persea*). See the illustrations on page 123 for techniques of pinching and pruning.

4. Pinching back is part of monthly care for fast-growing vining plants and plants like coleus, which become straggly if allowed to head for the ceiling.

5. Pruning is part of monthly care for plants that are being trained either to a topiary form or to climb a wall. See Chapter 7, in which both these subjects are covered in detail.

Staking and Training

1. Garden centers and five-and-dime stores sell various stakes; there's bamboo in several thicknesses, and soon we are promised attractive clear-plastic stakes in vinyl (I'm holding my breath!). For medium-size plants, use the medium-gauge bamboo, but for trees such as the weeping fig (*Ficus benjamina*), use 1-by-1-inch wooden stakes in dark green.

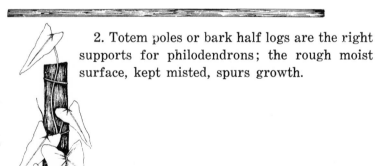

2. Totem poles or bark half logs are the right supports for philodendrons; the rough moist surface, kept misted, spurs growth.

3. When you place a support in the plant pot, set it carefully down between roots.

4. To tie plants to their supports, use twist ties which come in boxes or rolls of soft, fat, dark green wool.

5. Tie branches and trunks fairly loosely to the support. Don't contort or choke stems.

6. Supply centers offer ready-made trellises like the one illustrated here. They come in various sizes. Tie the plant branches to the cross sections as shown for the most effective support.

7. To train English ivy (*Hedera helix*) or creeping fig (*Ficus pumila*) to climb a wall, see illustration on page 125 and discussions on pages 124–126.

Propagation

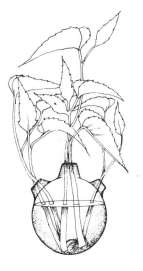

1. Propagating plants is fun, but office windows filled with odds and ends of plant limbs rooting in murky water don't look very businesslike. If you enjoy rooting plant parts, invest in good-looking glass globes to hang in windows. Plan a nice display and hang the globes on clear 40-pound fishing line. You can root cuttings in glasses and vases, too. They make attractive green bouquets.

2. Tip cuttings (pruned ends) 3 to 6 inches long of new or semi-new stems of many plants (I've noted the best to try in preceding chapters) root fairly easily when set in clear water or planted in moist-to-wet vermiculite or perlite. See the illustration on this page. To take tip cuttings, see the illustration in Chapter 5. The cutting is ready for potting in suitable soil when a mass of young roots shows in the glass or when a lot of vermiculite (a mini root ball) comes up when you tug on the cutting. Some tip cuttings root well

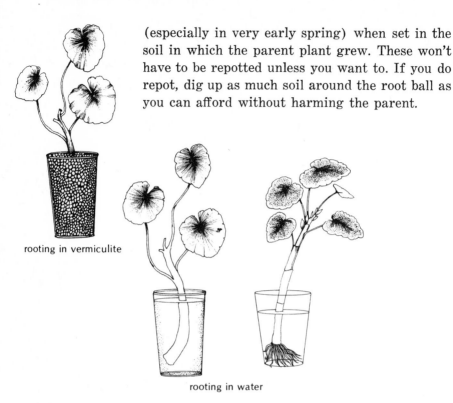

(especially in very early spring) when set in the soil in which the parent plant grew. These won't have to be repotted unless you want to. If you do repot, dig up as much soil around the root ball as you can afford without harming the parent.

rooting in vermiculite

rooting in water

3. Root division is a technique for dividing plants in order to get new ones. See item 8*j* under Soils, Potting, and Repotting, page 203).

4. Planting seeds is another way to increase your plant holdings and makes sense if you are on a budget and what is wanted is an easy-to-start item, such as the wax begonia (*Begonia semperflorens*). Fill an 8-inch pot or a peat flat (garden centers sell them) or lots of 3-inch pots with suitable soil and scatter the seed 1 or 2 inches apart over the surface. Cover with a sifting of soil, overwrap with thin plastic (like Saran wrap), water gently, and set in light indicated for the parent plant. When seedlings are up, remove the plastic; when they are 3 to 6 inches tall, pot as directed (see Soils, Potting, and Repotting, pages 201–203). You can also acquire wax begonias as illustrated by rooting tip cuttings.

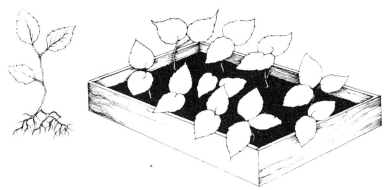

Roots form in propagating box or flat. Transplant into individual pots.

5. Air-layering is a technique used to turn leggy tall plants no longer beautiful into low new plants. Corn plant (*Dracaena fragrans*) is typical of plants that may need air-layering after a few years. To air-layer, follow the illustrations on this page; use the potting soil recommended for the parent.

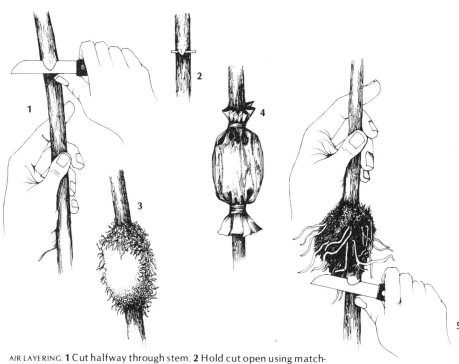

AIR LAYERING: **1** Cut halfway through stem. **2** Hold cut open using match-stick. **3** Surround cut with moistened sphagnum moss. **4** Wrap moss in plastic. **5** After rooting, cut stem below roots. Pot the new plant.

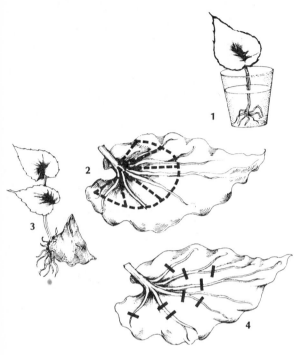

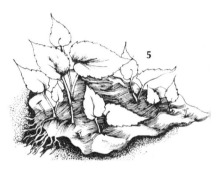

1 *Begonia rex* leaves may be rooted in water, then planted. 2 Dotted lines indicate where to cut. Include main vein in each wedge. 3 New plant from rooted wedge ready to be transplanted into pot from propagating medium. 4 On back of leaf, cut through veins as indicated by black lines. 5 Pin to moist propagating medium right side up.

    6. Propagation by leaf cutting is a technique applied to certain plants, such as African violets (*Saintpaulia*) and rex begonias (*Begonia rex*). See the illustrations on this page. Plant descriptions in chapters 2–6 tell which plants are best propagated by leaf cuttings.

    7. You can create instant big plants from fast-growing vining plants such as wandering jew (*Tradescantia*) by taking 6- to 12-inch tip or stem cuttings (same thing) of a lush parent plant and putting them together in a big vase of clean water. The cuttings will live there for months and can later be planted together in a new basket to replace a withering parent plant.

    8. Do not add plant food unless cuttings are living in water permanently.

    9. Cuttings usually take four to six weeks to root well. Keep the water clean. A chunk of charcoal (plant suppliers carry it) helps keep the water sweet.

Maintenance, Grooming, and Vacations

1. Systematic care is better than haphazard care.
2. Check your plants twice a week. Professionals allow 30

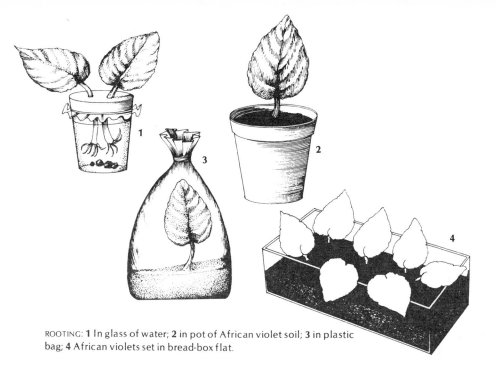

ROOTING: **1** In glass of water; **2** in pot of African violet soil; **3** in plastic bag; **4** African violets set in bread-box flat.

minutes weekly to care for two or three big plants or four or five small ones. Take the time to groom your plants and fuss over them a little. Then you'll have a chance to notice what is happening to them: whether they're growing or have suddenly stopped (repotting needed?), whether they have tiny holes or spots (insects?) or browning leaf edges (overwatering? not enough misting?).

3. A two-day maintenance system works well. Monday before work or during lunch, groom, mist, air, shower, spray, repot, pinch, prune, or do whatever else is needed to your plants. If small pots have dried out, water these. Thursday water all the plants, and give any additional care (misting and airing perhaps) that is needed.

4. Grooming means to remove any dead leaves, stems, or branches, including fading flowerbuds, and to trim away browning areas on leaves. See illustration on this page. It includes staking and cleaning the pot if needed. Constant grooming is the reason florists' plants always look beautiful.

5. Keeping a garden log has advantages. It encourages regularity in your care of the plants and allows anyone to replace you, leaving you free for vacations. (And it's fun.) In your log, enter each new plant; make a list of recommendations from preceding chapters for light, watering, misting, showering, fertilizing, pinching, spraying, repotting, and ways to propagate. Then note what you actually developed as a successful care pattern: how the plant responded, and date of repotting, etc. Note for flowering plants when bloom can be expected and how long it lasts.

If you are going on vacation and there is no one to water your plants, water well before you leave and tent them in clear plastic. Tuck the plastic in under the saucer so moisture can't escape.

tented pot

water—2 days
feed—15th of month
mist—daily
shower—
30th of month
prune—
15th and 30th

6. Make stickers for each pot noting watering, fertilizing, misting, showering, pinching patterns, and if you don't keep a log, make a notebook to match the stickers. This makes weekly maintenance easy and lets anyone take over plant care successfully.

7. If you leave a costly installation to go away on vacation, hire a professional to do maintenance.

8. Plants like vacations, too. A vacation can be a few weeks in a sunny spot in an office left empty by its owner. Another kind of vacation is a move outdoors. If you have an outside spot for plants in summer:

a. Move the plant into light similar to that it was in indoors.

b. Move plants only gradually into direct sun or they'll burn, even sun lovers like succulents.

c. Check pots for moisture daily outdoors, they dry faster.

d. Before you bring the plants indoors in late summer, spray for three weeks against white fly and red spider; the outdoors is buggy!

Problems and Solutions

1. Professionals check plants twice weekly for problems such as those listed in this section. They either spray plants as need becomes apparent or spray everything every two weeks, with all-purpose pesticide such as Malathion.

2. Notches in branches and undersides of leaves are where enemies often lurk.

3. Use all pesticides and solutions according to package directions. Since they are marketed under various trade names, it is impossible to give general instructions.

4. **White fly.** Ashlike specks on leaves and teensie things like dust motes that fly up when you move branches are symptoms of white fly. Heat and lack of air and humidity encourage them. Plants vacationing outdoors (or from poorly kept greenhouses) bring them in. Since the flies fly away when you approach, they're hard to do in. Spray with pesticide that specifically controls them or hang a no-pest strip in the area. Frequent misting and showering discourages attacks.

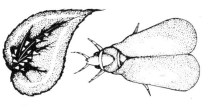

begonia leaf   white fly

5. **Red spider mite.** Worst of all indoor pests, it comes indoors through windows and on plants and plant materials. Symptoms are leaves that grow pale and have white or gray flecking. In time you'll see very fine spiderwebs. Sometimes you see the tiny red horrors themselves. Isotox is a good solution; Benlate or Benomyl also handle the eggs, a big plus. Fresh humid air discourages red spider.

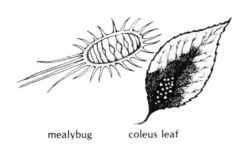

mealybug   coleus leaf

6. **Mealybugs.** Symptoms show as masses of cottony white eggs in branch crotches and under leaves. You can clean up the plant by swabbing bugs with alcohol-soaked cotton wrapped around a pencil tip, by washing affected parts weekly in warm soapy water, or by using a pesticide such as Malathion or Isotox. In amaryllis and many of the palms, eggs burrow between the leaves and are very hard to kill.

7. **Scale.** Ferns, ficuses, and palms are subject to scale—tiny tan or brown things found on stems and upper and lower sides of leaves. A sharp knife tip can pick away a small attack, but you'll need Malathion to treat a real infestation.

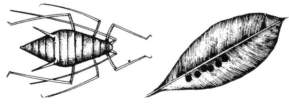

aphid   pittosporum leaf

8. **Aphids.** These are visible, tiny things, like pale-green eggs, which are hard to spot on the tender new growth they prefer. Washing every few days in warm soapy water may dispose of them, but if they persist, use Malathion.

fungus infection   begonia leaf

9. **Fungus infections.** These show various symptoms, usually soggy sunken areas, irregular brown patches (on rex begonias, for instance), and ugly blemishes on leaf surfaces. General-purpose Benlate or Benomyl handles a broad spectrum of fungus problems. If you have extensive plantings, consider a monthly treatment.

10. Professionals recommend against aerosol insect controls because of the fumes. A concentrated liquid or powder mixed with water and applied with a hand mister (kept especially for this purpose) is the best way.

11. If an infestation defies control, tent the plant with plastic (use cleaners' plastic bags Scotch-taped together), make an opening in the bag, and spray the plant. Leave the tent on half an hour or an hour, according to package directions on the pesticide.

12. White patches on clay pots is a result of mineral buildup. Scrub pots clean with steel wool or Brillo pads.

13. Moss on soil surfaces usually means overwatering and soil that is draining poorly. Repot.

14. Tender stems of African violets, for instance, resting on rough terracotta pot edges, get petiole rot. Remove dead leaves and repot in a bigger plastic pot.

15. Big basket plants showing lots of dead branches and leaves underneath probably are played out; they should be cut back and repotted. Use cuttings to start a fresh new plant.

Hiring Professional Help

1. If you are going to spend over $200, hire a professional indoor landscaper.

2. You'll find landscapers either in the yellow pages listed

under Landscapers, or under Plants. Or ask a local florist or greenhouse for a recommendation.

3. Get references and check them before you hire. Ask about their policy on guarantees.

4. Pros usually work three ways:

a. Consultation. About $25. They'll come to your office and tell you what plants to place where. A pool of the office staff can raise that much, and a pro can pull together plants you already have as well as keep you out of trouble when purchasing new ones.

b. Consultation plus installation. For 10 percent above the cost of the plants and installation equipment, they'll do the whole job. And maybe waive the consultation fee.

c. Consultation, installation, and maintenance. A landscaper who does maintenance usually will also give you a guarantee. A 30-day guarantee isn't particularly good. Two or three months is better.

5. Maintenance charges are about $15 an hour. Minimum is probably $30 a month. The highest maintenance fee I know is $900 a month for a large, fancy designer's office housing $12,000 to $15,000 worth of plants.

6. Average cost in New York for a modest reception area fully installed with plants is between $300 and $1,000. That includes containers for the plant pots, which can range from $10 apiece for simple baskets to $100 each for a fancy polished aluminum cube. Plants cost $10 to $15 per foot of height.

7. Price of maintenance contracts are governed by several factors: size of installation, size of plants, accessibility of plants, plants in groups versus plants singly all over the lot, durables versus exotics, $300 plants versus $50 plants, availability of water, etc. Maintenance includes labor to replace plants but not the cost of new plants, as a rule, unless your guarantee is operative.

Appendixes

A
Placement Service:
Light and Temperature
Requirements

These lists describe very generally light and temperature needs of the plants in this book and should be a help in designing gardens and in planning groups of plants that are to be in the same location. The light and temperature descriptions are general, since exact descriptions of each of the plants' light and temperature needs appear in chapters 2–6. As used here, B (for bright light) means usually that there is some direct sunlight reaching the plant, although a few of the plants can't take it for too long. F (for filtered light) means little or no direct sun is necessary to the plants and many can grow in fluorescent light or under desk lamps. W (for warm temperatures) means plants can take temperatures up to 78 or 80 degrees or higher. C (for cool temperatures) means temperatures 68 to 70 or 72 degrees are preferred, although many of the plants can take temperatures up to 75 degrees without harm.

HORTICULTURAL NAME	COMMON NAME	LIGHT	TEMPER-ATURE
Chapter 2: LITTLE PLANTS AT WORK			
Agave Species		B	W
Aglaonema Species	Chinese evergreen	F	C
Aloe Species	Unguentine plant	B	W
Ardisia crispa	Coralberry	F	W
Aspidistra elatior	Cast-iron plant	F	C
Asplenium nidus	Bird's-nest fern	B	C
Beaucarnea recurvata	Ponytail, Elephant foot	B	C/W
Begonia rex	Rex begonia	F	W
Cacti and Other Succulents		B	W
Calathea makoyana	Cathedral windows	F	C
Chlorophytum comosum	Spider plant, Airplane plant	F	C
Coleus Species		B/F	C

217

HORTICULTURAL NAME	COMMON NAME	LIGHT	TEMPER-ATURE
Crassula argentea	Jade plant	B	W
Cyperus alternifolius	Umbrella plant	F	C
Cyrtomium falcatum	Holly fern	F	C
Davallia Species	Rabbit's-foot fern	F	C
Dracaena sanderiana		F	C
Euphorbia Species		F	W
Ficus diversifolia	Mistletoe fig	B	C
Fittonia verschaffeltii argyoneura		F	C
Maranta leuconeura	Prayer plant, Rabbit tracks	F	C
Nephrolepis exaltata bostoniensis	Boston fern	F	C
Pellaea rotundifolia		F	C
Peperomia Species		F	W
Pilea cadierei	Aluminum plant	F	W
Plectranthus australis	Swedish ivy	B/F	C
Polypodium aureum mandaianum	Hare's-foot fern	F	C
Pteris Species	Table fern	F	C
Sansevieria trifasciata 'Hahnii'	Snake plant	F/B	C/W
Saxifraga sarmentosa	Strawberry begonia, Strawberry geranium	F	C
Tolmiea menziesii	Piggyback plant	F	C

Chapter 3: THE SHRUBS

Chamaedorea elegans 'Bella'	Neanthe bella palm	F	C
Chamaerops humilis	European fan palm	B/ss*	C
Cycas revoluta	Sago palm	B	C
Dieffenbachia Species	Dumbcane	B	W
Dizygotheca elegantissima	False aralia	B	W
Dracaena deremensis warneckei		F	W
Fatsia japonica and *Fatshedera lizei*		F	C
Ficus elastica	India rubber plant	B/F	W
Ficus lyrata	Fiddleleaf fig	B/F	W
Pandanus veitchii	Screw pine	B	W
Philodendron selloum	Cut- or split-leaved philodendron	B	W
Phoenix roebelenii	Pigmy date palm	B	W
Pittosporum tobira	Japanese pittosporum	B	C
Podocarpus macrophylla maki	Southern yew	B	C
Polyscias fruticosa 'Elegans'	Parsley aralia	B	W
Rhapis excelsa	Lady palm	B	C

Chapter 4: OFFICE TREES

Araucaria excelsa	Norfolk Island pine	F	C
Brassaia actinophylla	Schefflera, Queensland umbrella tree	B	W/C

* ss: some sun

HORTICULTURAL NAME	COMMON NAME	LIGHT	TEMPER-ATURE
Caryota mitis	Clustered fishtail palm	F	W
Chamaedorea erumpens	Bamboo palm	F	W
Chrysalidocarpus lutescens	Areca palm	F	W
Dracaena Species		F	W
Ficus benjamina	Weeping fig	B	C
Howeia fosteriana	Kentia palm	F	C
Persea americana	Avocado tree	F	C
Pleomele reflexa variegata 'Song of India'		F	W/C
Polyscias balfouriana and *P. filicifolia*		B/nds*	W/C
Veitchia merrillii	Manila palm	B/F	W
Yucca elephantipes	Spineless yucca	B	C

Chapter 5: CLIMBERS AND VINES

Asparagus densiflorus sprengeri	Asparagus fern	B	C
Ceropegia woodii	Rosary vine	F	C
Cissus Species	Grape ivy, Kangaroo vine	F/ss*	W
Ficus pumila	Creeping fig	F/B	C
Hedera helix	English ivy	B/F	C
Hoya carnosa	Wax plant	B	C
Passiflora Species	Passion flower	B	W
Philodendron oxycardium		F	W
Scindapsus aureus	Pothos, Devil's ivy	F	W
Senecio mikanioides	German ivy	F	C
Syngonium podophyllum	Nephthytis, Arrowhead plant	F	W
Tradescantia Species	Wandering jew	B	C

Chapter 6: COLOR AND BLOOM

Aeschynanthus speciosus	Lipstick vine	B	W
Begonia semperflorens	Wax begonias	F/B	C
Bougainvillea Species	Bougainvillea	B	C
Browallia	Browallia	F	C
Crossandra infundibuliformis	Crossandra	B	C
Hippeastrum	Amaryllis	B	C/W
Impatiens walleriana sultani	Impatiens	B	C
Kalanchoe blossfeldiana	Kalanchoe	B	C
Oxalis Species	Four-leaf clover plant	F	C
Paphiopedilum	Slipper orchids	F	W
Pelargonium hortorum	Geranium	B	C
Phalaenopsis	Moth orchid	F	W
Rhipsalidopsis gaertneri	Easter cactus	B	C
Rosa chinensis minima	Pigmy rose, Fairy rose	B	C
Saintpaulia	African violet	F/C	C/W
Spathiphyllum clevelandii	White flag	F	C/W
Thunbergia alata	Black-eyed-Susan vine	B	W

* nds: no direct sun

B
Evaluation Table

This table represents the thinking of several professional land-scapers on the subjects of durability of plants and their appeal.

HORTICULTURAL NAME	COMMON NAME	FOOLPROOF	EASY	LESS EASY	MOST BEAUTIFUL	MOST POPULAR
Chapter 2: LITTLE PLANTS AT WORK						
Agave Species			•		•	•
Aglaonema Species	Chinese evergreen	•				
Aloe Species	Unguentine plant		•			
Ardisia crispa	Coralberry	•				
Aspidistra elatior	Cast-iron plant	•				
Asplenium nidus	Bird's-nest fern			•	•	
Beaucarnea recurvata	Ponytail, Elephant foot		•			
Begonia rex	Rex begonia		•		•	
Cacti and Other Succulents			•			•
Calathea makoyana	Cathedral windows			•	•	
Chlorophytum comosum	Spider plant, Airplant plant	•				•
Coleus Species		•				•

HORTICULTURAL NAME	COMMON NAME	FOOLPROOF	EASY	LESS EASY	MOST BEAUTIFUL	MOST POPULAR
Crassula argentea	Jade plant		•			•
Cyperus alternifolius	Umbrella plant			•		
Cyrtomium falcatum	Holly fern		•			
Davallia Species	Rabbit's-foot fern			•	•	•
Dracaena sanderiana			•			
Euphorbia Species			•			
Ficus diversifolia	Mistletoe fig		•			
Fittonia verschaffeltii argyoneura			•		•	
Maranta leuconeura	Prayer plant, Rabbit tracks		•			
Nephrolepis exaltata bostoniensis	Boston fern			•		•
Pellaea rotundifolia				•		
Peperomia Species			•			•
Pilea cadierei	Aluminum plant		•			
Plectranthus australis	Swedish ivy		•			•
Polypodium aureum mandaianum	Hare's-foot fern			•		
Pteris Species	Table fern			•		
Sansevieria trifasciata 'Hahnii'	Snake plant	•				
Saxifraga sarmentosa	Strawberry begonia, Strawberry geranium		•		•	
Tolmiea menziesii	Piggyback plant		•			•

HORTICULTURAL NAME	COMMON NAME	FOOLPROOF	EASY	LESS EASY	MOST BEAUTIFUL	MOST POPULAR
Chapter 3: THE SHRUBS						
Chamaedorea elegans 'Bella'	Neanthe bella palm	●			●	
Chamaerops humilis	European fan palm		●			
Cycas revoluta	Sago palm			●		●
Dieffenbachia Species	Dumbcane		●	●		
Dizygotheca elegantissima	False aralia			●		●
Dracaena deremensis warneckei		●		●		
Fatsia japonica and *Fatshedera lizei*			●			
Ficus elastica	India rubber plant		●		●	
Ficus lyrata	Fiddleleaf fig		●			
Pandanus veitchii	Screw pine	●				
Philodendron selloum	Cut- or split-leaved philodendron		●		●	
Phoenix roebelenii	Pigmy date palm			●		●
Pittosporum tobira	Japanese pittosporum			●		
Podocarpus macrophylla maki	Southern yew			●		
Polyscias fruticosa 'Elegans'	Parsley aralia		●			●
Rhapis excelsa	Lady palm		●			

HORTICULTURAL NAME	COMMON NAME	FOOLPROOF	EASY	LESS EASY	MOST BEAUTIFUL	MOST POPULAR
Chapter 4: OFFICE TREES						
Araucaria excelsa	Norfolk Island pine		•			•
Brassaia actinophylla	Schefflera, Queensland umbrella tree		•			•
Caryota mitis	Clustered fishtail palm		•			
Chamaedorea erumpens	Bamboo palm	•				•
Chrysalidocarpus lutescens	Areca palm		•			•
Dracaena Species		•				•
Ficus benjamina	Weeping fig		•			•
Howeia fosteriana	Kentia palm	•				•
Persea americana	Avocado tree		•		•	
Pleomele reflexa variegata 'Song of India'		•				
Polyscias balfouriana and *P. filicifolia*			•			
Veitchia merrillii	Manila palm			•		
Yucca elephantipes	Spineless yucca		•			
Chapter 5: CLIMBERS AND VINES						
Asparagus densiflorus sprengeri	Asparagus fern		•			•
Ceropegia woodii	Rosary vine			•		
Cissus antarctica	Kangaroo vine		•			•

HORTICULTURAL NAME	COMMON NAME	FOOLPROOF	EASY	LESS EASY	MOST BEAUTIFUL	MOST POPULAR
Cissus rhombifolia	Grape ivy	•			•	
Ficus pumila	Creeping fig		•		•	
Hedera helix	English ivy		•			•
Hoya carnosa	Wax plant	•				
Passiflora Species	Passion flower			•	•	
Philodendron oxycardium		•				•
Scindapsus aureus	Pothos, Devil's ivy		•			•
Senecio mikanioides	German ivy		•		•	
Syngonium podophyllum	Nephthytis, Arrowhead plant		•			
Tradescantia Species	Wandering jew	•			•	
Chapter 6: COLOR AND BLOOM						
Aeschynanthus speciosus	Lipstick vine			•		
Begonia semperflorens	Wax begonias	•				•
Bougainvillea Species	Bougainvillea			•		
Browallia	Browallia			•	•	
Crossandra infundibuliformis	Crossandra		•			
Hippeastrum	Amaryllis		•		•	
Impatiens walleriana sultani	Impatiens		•			
Kalanchoe blossfeldiana	Kalanchoe		•			
Oxalis Species	Four-leaf clover plant			•	•	

224

HORTICULTURAL NAME	COMMON NAME	FOOLPROOF	EASY	LESS EASY	MOST BEAUTIFUL	MOST POPULAR
Paphiopedilum	Slipper orchids			•	•	
Pelargonium hortorum	Geranium		•			
Phalaenopsis	Moth orchid		•			
Rhipsalidopsis gaertneri	Easter cactus			•	•	
Rosa chinensis minima	Pigmy rose, Fairy rose		•			
Saintpaulia	African violets		•		•	•
Spathiphyllum clevelandii	White flag		•			•
Thunbergia alata	Black-eyed-Susan vine		•			

C
Mail-Order
Plant Suppliers

This is a very brief list of mail-order suppliers given to provide you with at least one name somewhere in your area you can appeal to for help in locating plants not found in local plant shops. There are many, many more mail-order growers. This is a limited list because of space. The fact that a supplier does not appear on this list does not in any way suggest that he is less than reputable. Since it is impossible to include here particulars of ordering for each supplier, it is a good idea to write for catalogs and other information before you place an order. Some growers have very handsome catalogs for which they charge a small fee. Well-illustrated catalogs are worth the small investment.

Alberts & Merkel Bros., Inc.
2210 S. Federal Hwy.
Boynton Beach, Florida 33435

Burgess Seed & Plant Co., Inc.
Box 90
Galesburg, Michigan 49053

Fuku-Bonsai
Box 178 Homestead Rd.
Kurtistown, Hawaii 96760

Hewston Green
Box 3115 PA-2
Seattle, Washington 98104
Catalog 50¢

Kartuz Greenhouses
92 Chestnut St.
Wilmington, Massachusetts 01887
Catalog $1.00

L. Easterbrook Greenhouses
10 Craig St.
Butler, Ohio 44822
Catalog $1.25

Logee's Greenhouses
55 North St.
Danielson, Connecticut 06239
Catalog $2.00

Merry Gardens
Camden, Maine 04843

George W. Park Seed Co., Inc.
Box 31
Greenwood, South Carolina 29646

Tinari Greenhouses
2325 Valley Rd., Box 190
Huntingdon Valley,
Pennsylvania 19006
Catalog 25¢

Index

Note: Bold type indicates pages on which entry is given most consideration.

Acclimatize, helping plants to, 192-193
Adiantum, 178
A. tenerum wrightii, 173
Aeonium haworthii, 168
Aeschynanthus speciosus, 142, **148**, 219, 224
African violet (*Saintpaulia*), 16, 19, 100, 140, **162**, 183, 219, 225
Agave, **25**, 110, 217, 220
A. filifera, 25
A. stricta, 25
A. victoria-reginae, 25
Aglaonema, **26**, 51, 217, 220
A. modestum, 18, 21, **26**, 81, 101, 106, 180, 217, 220
Air and temperature, 199
Airplane plant (*Chlorophytum comosum*), **36**, 101, 110, 126, 217, 220
Aloe, **27**, 110, 217, 220
A. aristata, 27
A. vera, **27**, 217, 220

Aluminum plant (*Pilea cadierei*), 42, **52**, 173, 218, 221
Amaryllis (*Hippeastrum*), 142, **153**, 219, 224
American wonder-lemon (*Citrus limonia* 'Ponderosa'), 70
Aphids, 212
Aralia ivy (*Fatshedera lizei*), **78**, 126, 218, 222
Araucaria excelsa, 96, 98, 218, 223
Areca palm (*Chrysalidocarpus lutescens*), 95, **104-105**, 219, 223
Ardisia crispa, **28**, 217, 220
Arrowhead plant (*Syngonium podophyllum*), 24, 125, 126, **137**, 180, 219, 224
Artillery plant (*Pilea microphylla*), 52, 173
Asparagus asparagoides myrtifolius, 126

light and temperature requirements, 217-218
selection of, 23-24
types of, 25-58
watering, 21-22
Lobivia, 33, 168

Madagascar jasmine (*Stephanotis floribunda*), 126
Maidenhair fern (*Adiantum tenerum wrightii*), 173
Mail-order suppliers, list of, 226
Malathion (pesticide), 211
Malpighia, 24
M. coccigera, 70
Mammillaria elongata, 33
Manila palm (*Veitchia merrillii*), 97, **113**, 219, 223
Maranta leuconeura, 35, **48**, 100, 170, 218, 221
M. leuconeura kerchoviana (rabbit tracks), **48**
M. leuconeura 'Manda's Emerald,' 48
Mealybugs, 212
Menninger, Karl, 12
Mini African violet (*Saintpaulia ionanthea*), 173
Mini creeping fig (*Ficus pumila minima*), 126, **130**, 173
Mini English ivy (*Hedera helix* 'Manda's Needlepoint'), 173
Mini maranta (*Calathea micans*), 173
Miniature *Begonia rex*, 170-171
Miniature *Begonia richmondensis*, 173

Miniature grape ivy (*Cissus striata*), 173
Miniature holly (*Malpighia coccigera*), 70
Miniature maple leaf begonia (*Begonia dregei macbethii*), 173
Miniature rose (*Rosa chinensis minima*), 142, 146, **161**, 219, 225
Mini-greenhouse (project), 185-186
Mistletoe fig (*Ficus diversifolia*), **46**, 176, 218, 221
Mistletoe fig (*Ficus lyrata*), 21
Monstera, 135
M. deliciosa, 82
Moth orchid (*Phalaenopsis*), 142, **159**, 219, 225

Names of plants, how to understand, 191
Natal plum (*Carissa grandiflora*), 70
National Council for Therapy and Rehabilitation through Horticulture, 12
Neanthe bella palm (*Chamaedorea elegans* 'Bella'), **71**, 96, 152, 173, 218, 222
Nephrolepis exaltata bostoniensis, **49**, 178, 180, 218, 221
N. exaltata bostoniensis compacta, 49
N. exaltata 'Fluffy Ruffles,' 49
N. exaltata 'Massii,' 178
N. exaltata 'Norwoodii,' 178
N. exaltata 'Rooseveltii,' 178
N. exaltata 'Verona,' 178

Unguentine plant (*Aloe vera*),
27, 217, 220

Vacations, maintenance of
plants and, 209-211
Variegated pothos (*Scindapsus
aureus*), 24, 100, 125,
135, 219, 224
Varieties, understanding, 191
Veitchii merrillii, 97, **113**, 219,
223
Vines, *see* Climbers and vines

Wandering jew (*Tradescantia*),
20, 52, 100, 124, 126,
138, 180, 219, 224
Water garden (project),
179-180
Water and watering, 10
climbers and vines, 124
color and bloom plants,
145-146
and humidifying, 196-199
little plants, 21-22
shrubs, 68
trees, 92

Watermelon begonia (*Peperomia sandersii*), 51
Wax begonia (*Begonia
semperflorens*), 140,
149, 219, 224
Wax plant (*Hoyo carnosa*),
123, 125, **132**, 185, 186,
219, 224
Weeping fig (*Ficus
benjamina*), 46, 80, **107**,
130, 176, 182
Weeping fig (*Ficus benjamina
'Exotica'*), 96, 97, 107,
176, 182, 219, 223
White flag (*Spathiphyllum
clevelandii*), 106, 112,
145, **163**, 219, 225
White fly problem, 211

Yucca elephantipes, 96,
114-115, 219, 223
Y. elephantipes 'Variegata,'
114

Zebrina pendula, 138
Zeitlin, Lawrence, 12-13
Zygocactus truncatus, 160